SACHIN Tendulkar
MASTERFUL

Peter Murray and Ashish Shukla

Rupa & Co

Published by

Rupa & Co

7/16, Ansari Road, Daryaganj,
New Delhi 110 002

Sales Centres:

Allahabad Bangalore Chandigarh Chennai
Dehradun Hyderabad Jaipur Kathmandu
Kolkata Ludhiana Mumbai Pune

ISBN 81-7167-806-8

Printed in India by
Ajanta Offset & Packaging Ltd
New Delhi

I N T R O D U C T I O N

It is hard to believe that in 1983 when I attended the Prudential World Cup in England that Sachin Tendulkar was only 10 years old. One can only imagine what it would have been like if Sachin had been in the victorious Indian team. Still, just 6 years later, he was representing his country and making a name for himself.

It was with great interest that I read about his first Test against Pakistan in 1989. I was keen to see what this superb young batsman would produce. I had read about his epic feat with Vinod Kambli in Bombay where the pair scored a 664 run stand while still at school and like so many cricket fans, I wanted to learn more about this young superstar.

Many years before Sachin was born, I was growing up in India and enjoying a beautiful childhood living in joyous cities such as Ambala, Nasik, Deolali and Bombay. My world of cricket was filled with names such as Sardesai, Durani, Manjerakar, Borde, Nadkarni and Pataudi - these were some of the stars of the 60's. Of course we all tried to emulate them and apart from playing cricket in school, we would visit the Maidans in Bombay every weekend to try and get a game. One got the feeling even then that many great names had graced the maidans and that many more would follow.

We left India in the late 60's like so many Anglo-Indians and migrated to Australia. At such a young age, it is difficult to comprehend a major life change let alone leave behind your friends, lifestyle and a thoroughly enjoyable way of living. We lived in Colaba - Bombay and I attended Cathedral High School - my father was an army officer who for most of my young life, was posted away. Being rather frail because of a major illness when young, my parents kept me away from sports - I would have to sneak away to enjoy cricket and football. I excelled in art, scripture and history and fought constantly against my "english" way of life. I wanted to know more... I wanted to enjoy all the Indian festivals and religious ways... I wanted to learn and play Indian music.. I wanted to eat rice and vegetables - not eggs and bacon... I wanted to become famous for playing the sitar or tubla for that matter... I wanted to see Indian movies - not the usual english movies... I wondered why my parents thought they were "English" when quiet obviously, we had all been born and brought up in India.

I arrived in Australia still full of questions - searching for the peaceful and serene life I left behind. Every opportunity I had to catch up on life back home was welcomed. Several years later in the late 70's, I decided to become a cricket writer after following the 1978 Indian tour in Australia where Chandrasekhar reached peak form to win the Melbourne Test for India against a virtually new Australian team. My first 'away' tour was to England for the 1983 World Cup when I was the editor of Cricket Lifestyle magazine. I arrived in London and promptly went to Lords to receive my accreditation and itinerary. I decided that this was a great opportunity to travel with the Indian team even though at the start of the tournament, India had very little chance of taking out the event.

This was the Indian team that included Mohinder Armanath, Roger Binny, Kapil Dev, Kris Srikkanth, Dilip Vengsarkar, Syed Kirmani, Sunil Gavaskar, Yashpal Sharma, Madan Lal, Ravi Shastri, Kirti Azad, Sandhu Singh and Sandeep Patil. My wife and I followed the Indian team to every event around England and I was lucky enough to be invited to several official functions. My biggest disappointment was when India played Zimbabwe at Tunbridge Wells on June 18 1983. Zimbabwe had scored 235 and got India into the precarious position of 7/78. Kapil Dev came out to bat and my wife suddenly took ill. We returned to London assuming that India had lost the match. To our surprise, the team arrived back in London with a victory - thanks to an incredible 175 not out from the Indian all-rounder Kapil Dev. From all accounts, this was an innings of pure pleasure.

Kapil cornered me at the next venue and accused me of "giving up on the team" by leaving early - he was only having me on. Throughout this tour, I became close to the team and in particular Mohinder "Jimmy" Armanath.

I had already met several of the players during previous Australian tours and felt completely at home. After this match against Zimbabwe, I started to feel that this Indian team could take out the tournament.

The day finally came - India versus the mighty West Indies at Lords. We were staying at the same hotel next to Lords as both teams and the night before the final, we attended both official dinners. India were relaxed and ready for the job ahead. The West Indies were 'cocky' and believed the Cup was already theirs. In fact, the ballroom at the hotel had already been booked by the West Indies team for their after win celebrations!

The rest is history. India took out the Championship and became hero's back home. I took the opportunity to visit India shortly after the tournament to launch my book on the event and took the time to catch up on lost years. Only 16 years had passed since I had left Bombay but it felt like a lifetime. I reflected on the stars of the 60's and felt privileged to know the stars of the 80's. I wondered who would be the stars of the next generation.

Close by, in Dadar, Sachin Tendulkar was being groomed to become India's and the World's greatest ever batsman. Like millions of Indians, I have followed Sachin's career with great interest. he has an aura or presence about him that very few have had before him and one can sense that the name Tendulkar will go down in history like Bradman and Grace. He is a superstar - a match winner and a team leader. Others can only follow in his wake.

With the help of my esteemed friend and renowned cricket writer Ashish Shukla, I have great pleasure in presenting this book to the many fans who have followed Sachin through his life and career. There is no doubt that with a possible decade ahead of him, Sachin will go down in history as the greatest ever.

I am privileged to be witness to the feats of Sachin Tendulkar. Let us all enjoy the life of this magnificent person and cricketer.

Peter Murray April 2002

THE EARLY YEARS

Dadar is a bustling place in Mumbai, not necessarily rich, but a nerve centre of a remarkable city nevertheless. Here, in Aagar Bazhar, an extremely crowded place even by Dadar's standard, lives Ramakant Acherkar. He rarely moves out of his home, inconvenienced as he is by a mild attack of paralysis, and very few visit him. One of those who does is Sachin Tendulkar, his most famous pupil. Tendulkar visits his coach before the start of every Test series, seeks his blessing and discusses cricketing points if any. The courteous regard he displays for his coach now is no different to the one he showed when he was first introduced to him.

It was a meeting which was nearly aborted. Tendulkar, was as nervous as hell and couldn't do a thing right in the presence of his imposing coach. Acherkar, unable to waste any further time on the youngster, suggested he come back six months later.

Tendulkar was downcast and devastated. As he was about to walk away dejected, his brother Ajit, who was convinced of his younger sibling's potential, asked Achrekar to have another look at young Sachin. After some persuasion, Achrekar agreed to let the kid stay but he insisted this second look would not last beyond a few days.

The day is vivid in Tendulkar's mind. "I couldn't bat normally at all. Coach said looks like this guy will take some time. But my brother said give him another chance and he agreed to keep me for seven more days."

Achrekar at this stage was a coach whose reputation was only limited to his own area of network. He was never an outstanding cricketer and played just one first class match, for all-India State Bank against Hyderabad in the Moin-ud-Dowla tournament in 1963-64. He used to work as the secretary of the New Hind Club in the mid-60s and his job included organising the club's cricket gear. Achrekar kind of drifted into coaching. One day he was buying some equipment from a sports shop, India Sports House, when a young boy entered the shop. The shop owner asked Achrekar if he could coach the young boy by the name of Suresh Shastri as the lad was a talented cricketer. Achrekar looked a natural in his new vocation and it so impressed the president of Arya Samaj - Mithailal Singh, that the latter offered to pay Achrekar to coach his son as well. Achrekar accepted a mere Rs 50 per month for his expenses but he soon became the coach of Dayanand Balak Vidyalaya, and it wasn't long before he was holding regular sessions at Sassanian Cricket Club on Azad Maidan. His career in coaching had started in earnest.

Achrekar had already put in nearly two decades in coaching when Tendulkar was first introduced to him. Tendulkar showed a remarkable passion for cricket at an early age and by 10 was batting with a cricket bat far bigger than him. Like most other Indian kids of middle class background, his initial cricket sessions were spent on the road - playing in the bylanes of Bandra, near his home, where weekend cricket is a community passion. When he was 11, he moved in with his paternal uncle to concentrate on cricket. It allowed him to be closer to the Shivaji Park area where coaching classes for young cricketers are held during summer vacations. Tendulkar took part in these camps but if he had any particular coach to guide him through, the world has not known it.

Under Achrekar, Tendulkar's life was now charted to a new course. His new coach's methods were simple and time-tested and demanded enormous discipline. Achrekar believed in putting his wards into match-situations and sometimes the young Tendulkar would play in as many as 13 matches in a day. In the huge Shivaji Park, where dozens of matches are held every Sunday, Tendulkar would get dismissed in one match and then promptly take a fresh guard in another closeby game.

Tendulkar's initial foray into matches was nothing to rave about. He was dismissed first ball in two matches. In the third, he managed seven runs for himself and felt on top of the world. He was pushed harder and harder by Achrekar in his new pursuit, practicing each day between 7 and 9 a.m. and 3.30 and 6.30 p.m. In between he would play matches. If Tendulkar fell for a low score in one match, his coach would take him to another game so he could bat again.

Recalls Achrekar: "In the process, Tendulkar sometimes found he played for about 13 different teams. One day when he was 14, he scored a century in the Giles Shield and then a double century in the Harris Shield."

Tendulkar's improvement was swift under Achrekar's methods. Achrekar would place a one rupee coin on top of the stumps and say "Anyone who gets him out will take this coin. If no one gets him out, Sachin is going to take it."

Tendulkar remembers to this day. "It was a big thing to get that coin for myself. I lost a couple of times but I have 13 coins with me. I didn't spend that money."

"At the age of 12 and 13 I was practising 12 hours a day. Seven till nine in the morning, then playing the game from 9.30 to 4.30 and then practising again from 5.30 to 7.00 in the evening. Once I played 54 matches in a row! My friends had music and films and I had cricket.."

Sure, the coach in Achrekar didn't approve of Tendulkar's bottom hand grip - probably a result of batting with a heavier and bigger bat while still small - but let him have his way as the results were encouraging. "More than anything else, I was keen for him to play his natural game. Yet I made sure he worked hard at his game. Practice, practice, practice makes a man."

Though batting was his forte, Tendulkar fancied himself as a fast bowler. He even took part in trials at the Chennai-based MRF Pace Foundation, to be trained under Australia's legendary fast bowler Dennis Lillee. "Very few know I had gone to Chennai for the selection by Lillee. I liked fast bowling, always have. I like watching them in action," states Tendulkar. He was gently turned away from his bowling ambition and asked to stick to his batting.

Tendulkar says the turning point in his career was changing school and moving to Shardashram Vidyamandir in Dadar - close to the Shivaji Park - on Achrekar's advice. It was at Shadashram school that he grew close to Vinod Kambli, another of Achrekar's pupils, and the two started demolishing bowling attacks at school level.

What brought Tendulkar to national consciousness was his unbeaten 664-run stand with Vinod Kambli for Sardhashram School in the inter-school tournament in 1988. Both got triple hundreds but it was a stand which almost didn't happen. As the two started belting bowlers around the park, the Tendulkar-Kambli duo noticed a man was waving from the boundary line with the coach's message to declare. But so enjoyable was the stint in the middle that the two young colts decided to ignore his coach's command. They got the firing of their life on return.

However, this partnership was momentous in more respects than one. It made headlines world over, even in publications as prestigious as Wisden. The Mumbai press, ever so eager to spot a talent and nurture it to the hilt, was full of praise for these two young men. Tendulkar was interviewed extensively, it was his first brush with stardom, and it ensured every innings of his from now on would not escape scrutiny. Tendulkar had arrived at the consciousness of Mumbai at least and it was only a matter of time before the well-oiled media machinery of the state would hoist him

on the national scene. Frankly, Tendulkar did not need any props. His talent was too awesome to be ignored. Past Test cricketers, of whom there are many dozens in Mumbai, would turn up at venues where Tendulkar was playing to have a look at the precocious young talent. Their bytes to media only added to Tendulkar's profile.

Dilip Vengsarkar, who briefly captained India in 1987-1988, said the members of the Indian team were surprised when he invited Tendulkar to play in the nets of the national team on the eve of an international match in Mumbai. "Frankly, many thought I was just being parochial. Their impression was that I was just trying to hoist a Mumbai teenager on to a bigger stage. It wasn't the case. Tendulkar appeared a genius to me at first sight. It was simply not possible for me to ignore him." Tendulkar attended the nets of the Indian team and sure enough, he received tremendous attention.

The decade of the 90s was one of cataclysmic influence in Indian cricket. For one, the cricketers had won an important legal battle with the Board of Control for Cricket in India (BCCI) and the official body was seething with rage under their breath. It so happened that after the Indian team, led by Dilip Vengsarkar, decided to halt in the United States and play a few "side" matches with a local promoter, and not return home from the West Indies where the team was involved in a Test series in 1989, the cricket board felt outraged enough to ban them from playing representative cricket for six months at least. The players decided to go to the courts and won an important battle where their rights to earn money as they deemed fit was upheld by the judiciary. Even though the cricketers won an important battle, the board was not the one to take the humiliation lying down.

The selectors, led by the suave Raj Singh Dungarpur, a former Ranji Trophy player, were keen to dump the players who had hauled the cricket body to court however opened the doors for the youngsters. Cricketers like Ajay Jadeja,

Sourav Ganguly, Subroto Banerjee, Venkatesh Prasad, Javagal Srinath, Anil Kumble, Vinod Kambli and Sachin Tendulkar suddenly found themselves thrust onto the national stage. What brought further attention to them was a string of A tours by foreign teams to India, including one from Pakistan, which received unprecedented attention in the Indian media. Though Tendulkar didn't play the series against Pakistan, as he was busy with his high school examinations, he had already been shortlisted for higher honours.

Dungarpur must be credited for giving Tendulkar the break his talent demanded. Says the high-profiled Indian administrator: "What I noticed about him was his cricketing acumen, besides of course the power he imparted in his shots. I remember watching him in a school game and he would repeatedly check his shot while driving to mid-off and mid-on so that he could pick up his singles." His cricketing acumen was already too sharp for his age. Years of playing maidan cricket, that is cricket played in unkempt grounds, had sharpened his instinct of match-play; the field placements, the strategies and tactics, Sachin Tendulkar had honed his skills sufficiently to impress the best.

Tendulkar was only 15 when he played first class cricket for Mumbai, then Bombay. In keeping true to the fairytale, he registered a century - a feat he was to repeat in his first appearance in the Deodhar and Duleep Trophy as well. While Ranji Trophy is the official domestic championship of Indian cricket, Deodhar is to assess the talents in the one-day arena and the Duleep Trophy is still a notch higher as it involves five days of intense cricket among the country's five zonal teams. The legend of Tendulkar was already on its way. Says Vengsarkar, who captained Tendulkar in his careers first first class game: "I remember a match we were playing in the South. The day was drawing to a close and on a crumbling pitch a rival spinner was proving almost

unplayable. Then it so happened towards the fag end, we lost wickets and it was now Tendulkar's turn to go out and bat. Since he was a top order batsman, I toyed with the idea of shielding him for the morrow and send a nightwatchman in instead. Tendulkar brushed aside the idea and the break which Tendulkar was waiting for finally arrived in 1989, on a tour to Pakistan of all places.

FIRST TEST KARACHI NOVEMBER 15-20, 1989

The selectors, presumably at the behest of higher ups in the board, were getting impatient to get even with the rebellious seniors. To compound matters, Vengsarkar said he needed a break after playing endless cricket for several seasons. The selectors jumped at the opportunity and made Krish Srikkanth the captain, to the surprise of many, since the cavalier Tamil Nadu opener was too buccannering and unorthodox to approach something as serious and solemn as captaining a national side. The side also included many youngsters, including two Mumbaikars, Salil Ankola and Sachin Tendulkar, and a new star in Sanjay Manjrekar. Tendulkar's inclusion generated a lot of interest since the young man was still not old enough to acquire a driving license. Indeed, since he was still not an adult, his contract with the cricket board was signed by his father and not Tendulkar. He still was under-age to perform the role! One needs to live in the sub-continent to understand the intensity and rivalry which cricket matches between India and Pakistan generate.

The players are charged up and their tense state reflects their every action and utterance. The two countries have gone to war on three occasions since their independence from British rule in 1947 and such hostility and cold diplomatic relations have meant the freezing of cricket relations from time to time. One particular cooling of period between the two countries lasted no less than 14 years before a diplomatic thaw saw the resumption of

cricket ties in 1977-78. There was a huge build up for this event and as the two sides were top heavy with stars and superstars, the build up to this series was awesome.

Bishan Singh Bedi, India's former captain, narrates an interesting incident. Bedi was the captain of the Indian team which toured Pakistan in the winter of 1978. He was also a regular in the county circuit in England where quite a few top Pakistan players were engaged for different counties. Bishan himself played for Northamptonshire which, in a remarkable coincidence, also had the services of Mushtaq Mohammad, the captain of the Pakistan side. Men like Zaheer Abbas, Sadiq Mohammad, Majid Khan, Imran Khan, Javed Miandad and Sarfraz Nawaz were all part of the County cricket set-up. States Bedi: "So great was the expectation that apparently top Pakistani batsmen were requesting that their fast bowlers, men like Imran and Sarfraz, go soft on them and don't bowl too many bouncers and beamers in county match-ups, lest they got injured and were deprived of turning up against the Indians." Zaheer Abbas, over a dinner with an Indian media party in the mid-90s, was to confirm the story as true.

The series was billed as a clash between world class Indian spinners and an outstanding Pakistani batting line-up. Pakistan also had some remarkable fast bowlers and everyone looked forward to their approaching contest against the Indian greats, Sunil Gavaskar and Gundappa Vishwanath. The Indian team also had a promising new fast bowler in Kapil Dev. Despite the hype, the series though was a one-sided affair as the Pakistani batsmen tore into the Indian spinning combination of Bedi and Prasanna, Chandra and Venkat and the visitors were left beaten 2-0 in a three-Test series. It generated a lot of bitterness, not the least because Mushtaq Mohammad was to declare the series win as one for "Islam." He even reportedly said the cricket matches against India in that series were a kind of "jehad"

for Pakistani cricketers. Bedi himself was so put off by a flurry of bouncers from Sarfraz at his batsmen in a one-day international that he conceded the game when in a winning position. He asserted it was in contravention to cricketing relations between India and Pakistan would then stumble from one disaster to another but still the 80s was a decade when the two sides played the most cricket against each other. Some memorable contests ensued, like the series in Pakistan in 1981 when Imran Khan and company literally blew away the Indian challenge, winning the six-Test series, by a 4-0 margin. Or one in India in 1987 when Pakistan, against all expectations, won the three-Test series by a 1-0 margin. India lost the final match at Bangalore by 16 runs, a defeat too bitter to swallow for the home fans. It was also the final Test of the legendary Sunil Gavaskar and befittingly, he made 96 in India's second innings which critics rate his greatest innings ever. The wicket had crumbled completely and Pakistan's spinners, Iqbal Qasim and Tauseef Ahmed were well nigh unplayable.

India were now to undertake a trip to Pakistan in 1989. Pakistan still had the services of Imran Khan and to boost their arsenal there was now a raw fast bowler of extreme promise, Waqar Younis. Not to miss the mercurial left-arm young paceman Wasim Akram who was already scorching turfs and making life difficult for international batsmen.

It was in these circumstances that Tendulkar was given his first Test cap for the first Test at Karachi, played on November 15-20, 1989. Also making his debut alongside him was Salil Ankola, a promising fast bowler. Pakistan too fielded a young tearaway Waqar Younis in their eleven who in days to come would be known as one of the greatest ever to have graced the game.

Tendulkar's turn to bat came on the second day of the first Test. His moment could have come on the first day itself had India's skipper Kris Srikkanth shown some nerve to bat

first after winning the toss. But the Indian team, trying to find its mooring under a new captain and with a largely young team, was not keen to take chances against a rival as formidable and bitter as Pakistan. Also, Pakistan's attack in the pace trio of Imran Khan, Wasim Akram and Waqar Younis, not to forget the leg spin wizard Abdul Qadir, was too potent to risk facing first up on the first morning of a Test on a fresh pitch.

Tendulkar, by all accounts, was tense and a little overawed by the names of those who were playing with and against him in this Test at Karachi. "I remember walking into the changing room and wondering how I would cope with all the famous names around me and they were all about twice my age. My captain, Krish Srikkanth was a great supporter. He sat me down before the game and told me that I belonged in the team, and they were all proud of my achievement. Nobody made me feel like a teenager."

At 16 years and 205 days, Tendulkar was the third youngest cricketer ever to play for his country in a Test match. Two Pakistanis were before him in the list of honour: Mushtaq Mohammad of Pakistan at 15 years and 124 days against West Indies in the Lahore Test of the 1959-60 series and Aaquib Javed at 16 years and 189 days when he turned out at Wellington against New Zealand in 1988-89. Since then the list has been completely revised. Now Hasan Raza at 14 years 227 days (vs Zimbabwe at Faisalabad in 1996-97) and Mohammad Sharrif of Bangladesh against Zimbabwe (at Bulawayo in 2000-2001) are at number one and three, pushing Tendulkar to number five in the all-time list.

Pakistan lost a wicket early but then built on steadily over the next few partnerships to reach 409 in their innings. Imran Khan himself hit a commanding century and almost every batsman in the top order got runs. The stylish Rameez Raja contributed 44, Shoaib Mohammad, one from the Mohammad stable, chipped in with 67 and the

irrepressible Javed Miandad himself would log 78 against his name. Saleem Malik, such a talented cricketer whose career was to end in such a shame in the late 90s on the match-fixing count, played attractively for his 36 runs. India were left to bat for nearly two sessions on the second day and Tendulkar had his first guard at the crease in Test cricket. By all accounts it was a baptism of fire.

It was not the first time in the match that Tendulkar was thrust onto centrestage. He was encouraged to turn his arm over during the Pakistan innings but 10 runs in his first over was as far as it lasted. Now his mettle would be tested against the fire and ferocity of the Pakistani fast bowlers. Was he frightened?

"I was too young at 16 to be frightened by anything. I went out to play as hard as I could. I dreamed of being the best player in the world, but you don't disclose that. I just wanted to score more runs than anybody else. I know now that it is mental discipline that sets people apart, the ability to think differently and to generate energy in the right direction. Everybody is trying hard; the players who succeed are the ones who push themselves a bit harder," states Tendulkar.

Tendulkar didn't have the cushion of a smooth platform when he walked into bat on the second afternoon of the Test. Wasim Akram was almost unplayable in his first spell and had the Indian openers out in no time at all.

Navjot Singh Sidhu departed in Wasim's first over, completely opened up by a big swinging delivery which rattled his stumps and then captain Srikkanth was adjudged leg before for four. Sanjay Manjrekar, who at the end of the series was the most remarkable player on either side, started the journey disastrously though as Waqar Younis now got into the act and had him snicking one behind the stumps for three. Manoj Prabhakar, looking to re-establish himself

in the Indian side after a gap of nearly five years, was Waqar's next victim, clean bowled for nine.

So Tendulkar walked out with the Indian board presenting a sorry sight at 4 for 41. The youngster was in a daze and didn't know what was happening around him. He was peppered by short-pitched deliveries by the rampaging Pakistani bowlers and realised instantly how quality cricket differed from school cricket and even a few domestic first class matches he had taken part in back home. He was also introduced to sledging as the home players tried their best to unnerve the youngster. After scratching together 15 runs, not in great style by a long definition, Tendulkar was cleaned up by Waqar as his third victim.

A teary-faced Tendulkar returned to the dressing room, unnerved by the hostile reception and the quality of the opponents. He doubted his own ability to stand up to this rigorous test. He later said he felt out of his depth in this class of cricket. India ended the day at 157 for six and were bowled out for 262 the next morning, conceding a lead of 147 runs. Almost the entire Pakistani bowling was handled by the pace trio who were in operation for 60 of the 72 overs bowled in the Indian innings. Qadir himself could get no more than 10 overs.

Pakistan ran up a total of 305 for five declared in their second innings, with Saleem Malik becoming the second centurion of the match. Shoaib Mohammad fell five runs short of it as the hosts raced to an imposing total - and lead - in just 96 overs. With a target of 453 in front of them, winning was out of question for India. They needed to bat a little over four sessions to save the Test. Fortunately, almost heroically, they were able to accomplish their aim, not because of Tendulkar but due to a very fine gritty unbeaten innings of 113 by Manjrekar. It was the start of a golden run for Manjrekar, son of Vijay Manjrekar, a distinguished, world class Indian batsman of the 60s, and he later went on

to get a double century in the series. India, at 303 for 3 when the match was abandoned as a draw, had covered themselves with credit. Unlike the first innings when Prabhakar and Tendulkar had batted ahead of him, it was Ravi Shastri who came in at number five and was still unbeaten with Manjrekar when the end came. Fortunately for Tendulkar, the dazzle of his talent was too obvious for the tour selectors to even think of dropping him for the rest of the matches. He indeed was made to feel part of the team from day one and had a sense of superiority when he could beat everyone in the team in arm-wrestling.

"He was too strong even at that age," recounts Vengsarkar, "He had so much strength in his arms and hands that none of us but Salil Ankola could beat him in an arm-wrestling duel on that tour." Vengsarkar also remembers how Tendulkar used to interact in monosyllables. "He was a very silent kind of character. Even then he used to be more of a listener rather than a talker. His brother would call him up from Mumbai and they would chat on the phone for a fairly long period yet the most one could hear from Tendulkar were some muted nods."

The famous characteristics of Tendulkar were evident this early in his career. Private and intense and extremely determined to succeed at the highest level. He was up and on his way with a half century under his belt in the next Test. It was also the Test when he was subjected to a barrage of verbal assault by Akram. According to an apocryphal tale, Tendulkar is said to have walked up to the fiery left-arm paceman and asked him why he had to sledge so hard when his bowling itself was in a class of its own. "After that half century, I knew I could survive at this level of cricket," says Tendulkar. Survive, he did.

FAMILY LIFE

The breakfast buffet at the hotel in East London South Africa was typical. Adults, with childlike impatience, trying to get ahead in the queue and help themselves to as much as they could. Expressions most sombre or full of pasted smiles, synthetic at the best of times, were like a mask for the eyes to target the next acquisition which would soon form the second tier of their already overflowing plates. At the very end of the hall sat a man with his back turned to the rest of the gentry, his left hand working quietly on the food on his table, nudging and prodding his two kids who flanked him to eat well. His striking wife, in the company of a maid, was facing this threesome from across the table.

It was a particularly long session, the man would get up now and then for a second filling, chatting incessantly with his wife in hushed tones while the kids forced attention with their antics. Years of living in the spotlight had taught the father that he could never be entirely private in public. Not, by a long shot, if you are an icon in the eyes of millions and millions of adoring fans.

Sachin Tendulkar was in East London with the rest of the Indian team to play a four-day game ahead of the second Test scheduled at Port Elizabeth, affectionately termed PE, a do-or-die affair in a three-Test series against the South Africans since the first one had been lost at Bloemfontein rather disastrously. The four-day fixture at East London was going nowhere because of the incessant rain and the poor quality of covers which the organisers had provided at the ground. Every morning cricketers would troop in in the breakfast hall - and then go back to their rooms to either sleep or watch television. East London didn't offer much by way of diversion. Cricketers and journalists would bump into each other at the breakfast table and then go their own way, only to repeat the scene the next morning.

Tendulkar and his family also stuck to their own routine. We, the journalists, left him in his own little private world, deferring to him as one would to royalty even as we back-slapped and cracked jokes with the rest of the cricketing squad. Over the years, the world has come to know how intensely private Tendulkar is. They all tend not to intrude, especially those who are in this game for professional and administrative reasons.

For a man who has had such a dramatic, often premature, development in his life, Tendulkar could appear pretty staid and dull in his private world. There is no preference for flashy clothes and lifestyle or a keenness to break into the inner circle of the film world - a typical trait of up-and-coming or even established Indian cricket stars. Quite a few have been irretrievably attracted to it, including the likes of Sandeep Patil, Mohammad Azharuddin, Salim Durrani and even the current captain Sourav Ganguly.

In India's entertainment world, nothing is bigger than cricket or films. It is only natural that stars of these two spheres seek acceptance and respect in each other's area of influence but Tendulkar has shown no such frailty in his temperament. He would rather spend time with the people he has grown up with or his immediate family.

The third son of four siblings, three brothers and a sister, Tendulkar was born on April 24, 1974 to Ramesh and Rajni Tendulkar in a quiet, unpretentious locality of suburban Mumbai. His father was a Marathi poet and a writer who earned his living as a professor first in the Siddharth College founded by Dr. B. R. Ambedkar, and later in the Kirti College in Mumbai. His mother worked for the Life Insurance Corporation - India's ubiquitous state-controlled giant of an insurance company. It is a measure of importance they attached to values, as stressed by a whole lot of ordinary middle class Indian parents, that even after

their youngest son had become rich and famous, both Ramesh and Rajni quietly kept up the schedule they had followed with such discipline and dignity for decades.

The eldest of the Tendulkar klan is Nitin who works for Air India. Ajit, the second brother, is credited with introducing Tendulkar to the cricket field. The influence of Ajit shows no sign of abating in Sachin's life. The young genius still turns only to his immediate elder brother while discussing a cricketing strategy or a particular nuance of his batting. He has no doubt that Ajit offers sound cricketing advice as any past or present international cricketer or renowned coach he has had during his distinguished career. Ajit also looks after the day-to-day business affairs of his younger brother. Tendullkar feels nobody knows his game better than Ajit. His only sister, Sampada Palekar, is married and lives in Pune, Maharashtra.

In human lives, a child's parents are his first heroes. As he gains in years, the impression dilutes. The influence of the world, the people he interacts with, his own impressions and if he is fortunate enough to travel - unleashes a free spirit which is more critical and sceptical and tends to view men and matter with more than a little reservation. Tendulkar was exposed very early in life to a world far beyond the scope of imagination of his elders and as he became successful, he too was surrounded by self-seekers and those who wished to massage his ego. He was a celebrity while still in his teens, his pictures and interviews would peer down at viewers and readers in India's newspapers, magazines and television channels, and his massive fan-following was reflected every time he set his foot outside the threshold of his house. The papparazzi, the shrieking fans, the clamour for his autograph was growing all the time. Tendullkar always seems to take it in his stride and will never lose his cool in public.

Did he ever suffer from the bouts of meglamania which a celebrity at least once succumbs to during his years of stardom? For a man on whom the pressure of stardom is more intense than it would be even on a Michael Jordon or Tiger Woods, it is only human if he believed he is the chosen one, a particularly valuable god's gift to mankind. Sure, Tendulkar felt heady at times. He made a rare, even touchingly human confession to yours' truly recently. "It is only human if sometimes you are taken in by such reactions from the world at large. Whenever I would get a little astray, I always would be pulled back in line by the people around me, those whom I trust completely."

If Tendulkar could handle his fame like very few have in today's world of unprecedented glamour and commerce which surrounds a sporting celebrity, it is largely because of his background. At least he has little doubt on the matter. "I think it is my background, the typical middle class virtues of an Indian home, which has shaped me as a person," commented Tendulkar.

The elder Tendulkar was more than a father to Sachin. The relationship extended far beyond the one of father and son. Tendulkar seemed to identify with the spirit of his father which he often refers to as one of immense "inner calm." The values within the four walls of Tendulkar's household almost entirely were coded with the tenets of moral virtues. An obsession with money or worldly matters was thumbed down. It was important that you were seen sticking to grace and honour in every living day of your life.

Unlike his father, Tendulkar was never a man of letters. By all accounts he was not a bright student at school. He was already inclined towards cricket; when India won the 1983 World Cup, Tendulkar, then 10, became obsessed with the game. Still, he somehow managed to clear his school board examination and joined Kirti College, where his father

taught, for his university education. The elder Tendulkar wasn't particularly interested in sport, but he was always supportive to Sachin and never put any pressure on him. "Whatever you do in life, be sincere and honest was his credo," reflects Tendulkar now. Tendulkar would touch the feet of his parents before playing any match in Mumbai, a practice he followed even after he had become an international icon.

Sachin grew up in Sahitya Sahawas Colony, a typical colony of writers in Bandra, Mumbai where youngsters would get together in the park to discuss the title of a book rather than exchange notes on their boys or girlfriends. A typically quaint and laidback colony, Sahitya Sahawas afforded Tendulkar an opportunity to access homes, trees and playgrounds. He, photographer Avinash Gowariker and contractor Sunil Harshe formed a trio of unrestrained energy. "One Sunday while everyone was reading the movie Guide, Sachin and I found ourselves on the same branch of a mango tree," says Sunil, "It broke - sending us down with a thud, which alerted an elderly neighbour, and we ran for our lives."

The summer vacations only prolonged their hours of antics and playful mischief. They played cricket and a host of other games like viti dandi and shigrupi. Sachin lay in wait for the kill while playing hide-and-seek. He would hide when it was his turn to seek, waiting for the others to come out, so he could catch them.

Sahitya Sahawas was still being built those days and the boys delighted in making booby-traps in the mounds of sand and bricks lying around. They also flitted around on a rented bicycle but there were still extra calories to be burnt. And this Sachin did with physical fights: whenever he was introduced to a new friend, Sachin would challenge him to beat him. Very few could do that. Besides cricket, he was

also a great tennis fan and used to back American tennis great John McEnroe while the rest of his friends in the colony supported Bjorn Born. "McEnroe has always been my hero, and he still is. I used to roam around with a head band, sweat band and tennis racquet imitating him."

Even though Sachin was playful and often mischievous, he was capable of deep affection and could be very sensitive. Remembers Sunil: "Playing 'dummy' on a summer evening in Sachin's house we were hiding under blankets and he was to identify us by touch. He wouldn't let us switch on the fan even though it was very hot. He was afraid that the pigeons in the nest would get hurt."

While his parents worked, Sachin was looked after by his nanny, Laxmibai, now over 70. She looked after him for 11 years. "he was a wonderful child, very mischievous and extremely restless. He would take a box and play the dhol (drum) and sing loudly like a joker," recounts Laxmibai.

"Even as a toddler, Sachin was attracted to cricket. When he was two and a half years old, he used to insist that I throw the ball at him. It was a plastic ball and he batted with a dhoka (washing stick)," says Laxmibai "We used to go to the terrace and play. I was the first bowler he faced in his life. His first cricket bat was gifted to him on a birthday."

Continued Laxmibai: "After coming home from school, he used to have his milk very reluctantly on the staircase. At times, he would give the milk to Ramesh, his childhood friend who is now his secretary. I used to feed him while he played." Sachin always insisted on two plates, one for him and another for Ramesh, whose father was a watchman. At times the two boys ate from one plate.

Sachin loved fish beside mutton chop with egg. "At times, I used to buy fish with my own money and cook for him and

his brothers," says Laxmibai "Sachin and his brothers would say that they would hang my photograph in their house after my death.

Sachin used to visit Laxmibai's house at Khar Danda to look at the sea. "Once he came for my granddaughter's birthday. He chased the hens around the house," says Laxmibai.

Laxmibai insists Tendulkar hasn't changed. "Whenever he sees me on the road near Sahitya Sahawas, the colony where Sachin lives, he stops the car and comes to me. He places his hand over my head and pats my cheeks. He hasn't changed. He is still like my son."

Sachin's nanny was a special invitee to his wedding. His brother Ajit and close friend Sunil Harshe went to pick her up in their car. "Both Sachin and his wife Anjali touched my feet. I was moved. I bless him even when I watch his matches on TV."

One person who never watches Sachin play, not even on television, is his brother Ajit. It is quite ironic the man whose sole mission was to see his younger brother succeed in the cricket world, can't bring himself to actually watch him in action.

"It has become quite a joke, because we can never find him when he knows I have to play a big innings. I scored a hundred in a school match and he has not been back since. Somebody rings him up after I have played to tell him what I've done and then he'll watch it on tape."

Word is still not out in public as to how the affair between Anjali and Sachin blossomed and culminated in their marriage. Anjali, a practicing pediatrician who works at the JJ Hospital in Mumbai, is at least four years senior to her

husband. Daughter of an industrialist father and British mother, Anjali has an easiness about her which compliments Tendulkar perfectly. Their marriage some six years ago was a much-anticipated event in India and television companies outbid each other to secure the television rights of the event. Tendulkar though was not to be dissuaded, money was of little consideration to him - only his privacy which must be guarded with utmost vigil. Only a select few were invited to the gala function. Most were kept out of bounds by the tight security cover which Tendulkar had invoked for the event. Sara, now in her fifth year, is the elder of Tendulkar's kids. Son Arjun has inherited his father's famous curly hair.

Anjali has been a source of strength in Tendulkar's life. She has been a support and not a hindrance in Tendulkar's pursuit for still greater heights in his career. The two kids are being brought up without any tantrums. Unlike kids of the rich and famous, Sara and Arjun are allowed to mingle freely with neighbours children, even with those of helpers, and there is no stifling do's and dont's for them - as is usually the case with people in exalted places who fear for their kids security and worry about the corrosive influence of interaction with people of lower status.

The media has fallen over each other to secure interviews of people who form his family. They haven't succeeded so far. There has been no interview of his father while he was alive, or his mother or for that matter his brothers and sister. Requests to interview his wife are always met with a definite no. There are rumours he was pursued most vigorously to give his consent for a television interview along with his wife to a show hosted by former actress Simi Grewal, a kind of Oprah Winfry presentation minus the audience, but nothing came out of it.

Tendulkar would lend his face and presence for a cause, not for a public exhibition of his private self. It is a credit to his family too who have avoided the temptation to bask in Sachin's limelight.

His taste and preference in the matter is best illustrated by an incident. When his daughter Sara was born, the entire spectrum of the Indian media wanted to be the first with her photograph. There was no way Tendulkar would allow it. It so happened the late Mark Mascarenhas, promoter of Tendulkar, once invited a reporter of a national magazine to his sprawling home in the United States at a time when the Tendulkars were also vacationing in the place. The reporter, true to his profession, succeeded in snapping Sara with Anjali and Sachin and sure the picture and the story was there in the next issue of the magazine. Tendulkar, his close ones insist, was extremely put off at this intrusion in his private world. Even now when Anjali visits Tendulkar on a tour with the kids, the Indian photographers curb their natural instincts and leave the Tendulkars in their own private world. If at all some photographs are taken, they adorn the private albums of the Tendulkars and are never exhibited in public.

It is this atmosphere of complete trust and lack of envy, pride or ambition on the part of his immediate family which has kept Tendulkar's feet firmly planted to the ground. They treat him as they have always treated him and Tendulkar is grateful for that. For many years, Tendulkar stayed in the same house as his parents. A little later, he allowed himself to shift to a different floor but that too in the same block as the one in which he grew up and now where his parents live. Only recently, has he shifted to a bigger house but it too is not very far off. He prefers to be close to Sahitya Sahawas which affords him the freedom to move around as he wants without being mobbed; here he is allowed to have his own emotional space. Anjali attends all

functions in Sahitya Sahawas and daughter Sara's first birthday on October 12 drew all the children and their mothers in the colony to the Tendulkar home.

All this points to an amazingly human face which Tendulkar has and reflects well on the family bonds and virtues of his intensely private world. Here money and fame take a backseat. Humility is very important. Like a karmic sadhu, Tendulkar suggests an extreme detachment from the fame, glamour and money which surround him. You would find him the least vocal in the team's net sessions, a team man to the core many youngsters in the past few years have looked up to him for guidance. A Harbhajan Singh would point out how he has taught him to spin with a new ball; a Shiv Sunder Das would acknowledge readily how his technique against short, rising deliveries was smoothened by Tendulkar's guidance; a Virender Sehwag is always at hand to let you know how benefiting is the master class of the little icon.

Faith is central to Sachin's psyche. A firm believer in God, he frequents the Shivaji Park Ganesh mandir, and his cricketing kit has an embossed image of the Lord. Recalls Professor Ratnakar Shetty, a high-profile official of the Mumbai Cricket Association who was manager of the Indian team which toured Sri Lanka in 1997. "After we had done badly in Sri Lanka, Sachin and I had planned to visit the Ganapati Temple at the GSB Hall in Wadala. As he had to go to Toronto to play against Pakistan, I visited the temple on our behalf. When India won 4-0, Sachin called up from Canada and thanked me for visiting the temple." Tendulkar says he visits temples at night when it is not crowded and is peaceful. Ganapati and Sai Baba are two of his favourite dieties and he believes his talent and success is all because of God's grace.

"It has been harder for my family than for me to be honest; I've known no other way. A couple of times I tried going out for the evening in disguise but that didn't work too well, so now I just stay in," he smiled. "Now, when I go to pray I go late at night to the temples which are empty and quiet."

Sachin simply loves music. He has a vast collection of western pop and serious music and spends his free time listening to his favourite artists on his fabulous music system. He also has a taste for perfumes and sea food. It is not as much the quantity but the finesse with which the food is served which defines his appetite. He would like his food to be well-made and served with all the essential props and side dishes. He is also a good cook himself. On one occasion while a match was being played in Delhi he visited team-mate Ajay Jadeja's home and cooked baigan-bhartha (a brinzal dish) for the rest of his team-mates. He also loves his car and keeps fidgeting with its machinery.

CRICKETING ICON

TEST CAREER

"It kept too low." Sachin Tendulkar had just seated himself beside me. The driver had eased the black sedan out of the parking lot of the majestic Taj Palace Hotel in New Delhi and we were heading for a private dinner. His mutterings were as incongruous as the protection of just a mustard cotton shirt he was wearing on a cool wintery evening. He spoke of an opportunity lost, full of dark forebodings and the night appeared to have grown darker.

India had finished the second day of the second cricket Test against Zimbabwe in Delhi's Test venue, Ferozeshah Kotla, at 171 for four. Matching Zimbabwe's 329 was now in the realms of fantasy. Tendulkar himself was dismissed for 36 in the final minutes. He was much tormented by the left-arm spin of Raymond Price, a little known left-arm spinner who has far too many lines on his rather craggy face which, with his unkempt blonde patch of hair and hostile eyes, gives him a rather sinister look at the crease.

Tendulkar was pained by his dismissal, couldn't see how India was going to haul itself on an even keel or dare to look at the target which India would face in the fourth innings of the match on a pitch which had crumbled in a heap of dust and scruffed footmarks. "I have a funny feeling about this game now," said Tendulkar. He appeared too faraway to respond to my cheerful suggestions.

But then cricket is just not a game for him. Approximately 20,000 international runs from nearly 400 representative games later, Tendulkar says his intensity is the same he felt in his veins as when he first walked on to a Test pitch, against Pakistan at Karachi a full 13 seasons ago. His preparation for a game is almost legendary. He indulges in

mental rehearsal against the bowlers and the pitch he is to contend with the next day and is unable to sleep at all on the eve of a Test. He wants to eliminate all possibility of a failure, as if it would discredit him in his own eyes. A man who can't walk in the open or live within his own four walls without somebody asking for his time and attention at all times, still finds time to keep his affair with batting going with the same intensity when the world was still to grow up on a callow youth.

His best knocks have spanned the entire length of his career. He didn't need time to grow into the harsh environs of international cricket. Somehow, he always looked prepared to take on the world's best in unfamiliar conditions. Imran Khan, Wasim Akram and Waqar Younis in his first series, Richard Hadlee in the next, Merv Hughes, Craig McDermott, Paul Reiffel and Allan Donald on the subsequent tours couldn't dislodge a young boy of 15 from his journey to be a cricketing icon.

He was into his third year of international cricket, still a teenager at 18, when India took a tour to Australia. It is not often India tours Down Under, only once in a decade and it's because England or West Indies always seem a better draw for the home audience. India has won only two Tests in its history against Australia while touring and both of them came when Australian cricket were busy raising a bunch of unknowns to fill in the void created by the desertion of top stars to the Kerry Packer circus in 1978. Now, in the early 90s, the fortunes of these two cricket teams were riding sky high. India had much to recommend by way of star value - Mohammed Azharuddin had just a year ago smashed a hundred at Lord's - preceded by an equally dazzling 192 against New Zealand at Auckland - which was one of the best ever seen at the holy turf and put to shade a stupendous 333 by Graham Gooch in England's first innings. Sanjay Manjrekar was another top gun who had taken a double hundred off Imran Khan, Wasim Akram

and Waqar Younis. Australia, on their part, were very much at the height of the Border era. They had some outstanding batting talents in Mark Taylor, Dean Jones, David Boon, Geoff Marsh, Allan Border and wicketkeeper Ian Healy. The bowling attack of McDermott, Hughes and Reiffel was well supplemented by allrounder Tom Moody. They were on the threshold of a golden era what with the Waugh brothers just beginning to get noticed and the exceptionally talented Shane Warne making his Test debut - however inauspicious - in the third Test at Sydney.

The pre-series billing proved a misnomer though as Australia raced to a 3-0 lead by the time the fourth Test in Adelaide was over. The blistering pace attack ripped open the much vaunted batting line-up. Azhar, Vengsarkar and Manjrekar through a mixture of failure to come to terms with lively attacks on quick tracks and thus low on confidence were now a liability. Openers K. Srikkanth and Navjot Singh Sidhu proved wholly inadequate to the task and Ravi Shastri, impressive with his double century on a placid Sydney track, had flown back to India because of a recurring knee injury. Only Kapil Dev and Prabhakar with 43 of the 73 scalps their way, seemed to push Australia back into their trenches at times.

Thus there was a bit of an inevitability when the two teams lined up for the fifth Test on a hot day in Perth. India lost the toss but began well in the field to account for openers Mark Taylor and Wayne Phillips with only 21 on the board. Allan Border and David Boon were cautious but unseparated till the lunch-time score of 53 for two. Border raises 59 for himself and a century stand with Boon before he became Kapil Dev's 399th Test victim at the stroke of tea.

India accounted for Dean Jones in the final session but Boon was still unbeaten on 92 and Moody on 42 in the team total of 4 for 222 when stumps were drawn. The hosts raised 346 for themselves on the second day, Boon got to his

fighting century and Prabhakar's perseverance was rewarded with five wickets for 101 runs.

India were in trouble straightaway when Sidhu departed to the Hughes - Healy combination for five. His partner Kris Srikkanth, after an entertaining yet torrid progress to 34 was the next one to go and when Manjrekar left yet again in the 30s, India were three down for 100. It soon was to become 4 for 109 when Vengarkar became Hughes' third victim for one. McDermott picked up his second scalp when Azhar hung his bat out at 11 and India at 5 for 130 appeared all but humiliated once again.

Tendulkar, meanwhile at the other end, was building a little masterpiece for himself. He hit a four now and then, survived a close call for leg before against Hughes off a full-pitched slower delivery. The young colt ended the first day unbeaten on 31, with nightwatchman Venkatapathy Raju on one in the team's total of 5 for 135.

Raju was gone without adding any on the third morning to Mike Whitney but the Tendulkar-Hughes contest at the other end was an engaging spectacle. Hughes with his chest free of any restrain from shirt buttons, many pounds of flesh seemingly hanging out of his awesome frame, a growling visage heightened by a walrus-like moustache, pounded away his full repertoire at the baby-faced youngster. Tendulkar, unlike on the previous day, was in a mood to dominate. He cut the Victorian fast bowler for a four and continued to play his shots till he reached his half century. His senior partner Kapil Dev stays long enough to stretch the score to 7 for 159 though his contribution was only four runs. Prabhakar didn't trouble the scorer and his cut was held at fourth slip off Whitney to make India eight down for 159.

Tendulkar is now left with only wicketkeeper Kiran More and Javagal Srinath to do what he can for the team. He

watched More play Reiffel up in the air but forward of point for two and then lost the next ball completely but the gloved chance fell just short of Boon. It's a signal for Tendulkar to abandon caution and let his aggressive instincts reign. He is lucky to find a flick off Hughes just elude Healy down the legside for a four and three more runs in the over make him go past Shastri as the highest scorer for India in the series.

He survives a chance at 73, only technical though, as Boon at forward short leg intercepts a hard push off Whitney. At the drinks break, India are 188 for eight with More shielded completely from the pack of bowling hounds.

The second hour of the day was Tendulkar's in every macrosecond of the term. He brought a rousing climax to an innings which would be hailed as one of the greatest ever seen Down Under. Men many years his senior wouldn't dream of a counterattack this belligerent and breathtaking against an awesome attack on a designer pitch. He had a near thing when he let one go from Whitney which struck his pads and was almost dragged back onto his stumps but didn't come back enough to hit the stumps. A booming cover drive for four with a single to end the over retained him the strike.

Runs were now almost completely being scored by Tendulkar. When Reiffel bowled a no ball to bring up the 200 of the innings, it was a long time since a run had come without Tendulkar's bat coming into the picture. A four and three in this over took Tendulkar into the 90s. The Aussies were now intent to deny Tendulkar the strike, the bowling reshuffles are done almost every over to break his rhythm - when skill fails, the mind-games come into play - this seems to be the policy.

Tactically too the Aussies show their characteristic alertness. Reiffel bowls bouncers to end an over and denied Tendulkar retention of strike. More was now left to face

McDermott and indeed struck a boundary to raise 50 for the stand in just 53 minutes. Tendulkar now has a full over to face from Reiffel and a brace with three from the last ball brought him tantalisingly close to his hundred. McDermott's first ball from the other end settled the issue with Tendulkar striking a four. An outstanding innings of three and a quarter hours, with 14 fours from 135 balls, is almost divine in its scope and breadth. In all 98 runs are added in the opening session and Tendulkar's contribution is 81 to More's 11. India are 8 for 233 at the lunch break.

Tendulkar departed almost immediately after lunch when his defensive prod was unable to beat the angle of a Whitney delivery from taking an edge and landing into the hands of Moody at second slip. The Aussies in the field seemed to clap endlessly, in a certain formation if one might add, and the generous crowd at the WACA are up on their feet in acknowledgement of a wondrous innings from a lad with so few seasons behind him. The roar followed him into the pavilion where his team-mates, some old enough to be his father, were dazed and speechless mindful they had just seen a masterpiece created in front of them. It was a privilege to be at the WACA that day, more so if you wore the same colours and shared the same nationality. A pity, not many Indians saw any merit in travelling to Perth, a country away from a country so far is it from the traditional city centres of Brisbane, Adelaide, Melbourne and Sydney of Australia.

The rest of the match was predictable but nobody seemed to notice Australia run up a big second innings total and then stop India well short of the set target of 442 to win the match. India folded up for only 141, Tendulkar contributing all of four, but the cricket world in general had found its reason to remember the match. It was Tendulkar's game out and out. In days to come, the little lad would be hailed as the next Bradman - by none other than the Don himself.

India in the 90s was a team in transition. Seniors like Kapil Dev, Dilip Vengsarkar and Ravi Shastri were on their way out. Manoj Prabhakar, hugely talented but a difficult team man, was on a voyage of self destruction. Talented cricketers such as Vinod Kambli and Subroto Banerjee belied their early promise. Sanjay Manjrekar was never the same batsman after Merv Hughes psyched him into submission in the Australian summer of 1991. Mohammad Azharuddin, now firmly in the saddle through victories in the home series, built on the two pillars of Tendulkar and Anil Kumble, was carrying his own agenda. "Azza" didn't like the presence of seniors in the side and his (ill) treatment of Navjot Singh Sidhu, Prabhakar and Kapil Dev is pretty well-documented. By 1996, Kapil Dev and Prabhakar were out of the picture and Sidhu was hurt enough to leave the touring party in a huff, before the three-Test series against England.

This series was to have a defining significance in the context of Indian cricket. The winds of change were blowing stronger than ever. India, humiliated by Sri Lanka in the 1996 World Cup semi-finals at Eden Gardens, was in a mood of retribution. Someone needed to be held accountable for India's embarrassment. Azhar paid the price after India lost 1-0 to England in the series. The Sidhu episode didn't do him any credit, nor his own form and his brazen affair with an Indian film actress was the stuff of bad publicity which Indian cricket could ill afford.

Tendulkar, meanwhile, was looking more lustrous than ever. He had an outstanding world cup and his century in the first Test at Edgbaston more or less unofficially anointed him as India's future skipper.

This hundred at Edgbaston was a remarkable innings in its own right. It was Tendulkar's ninth century at the tender age of 23 and no-one doubted he was the most outstanding right-hander in the game at that moment. The Telegraph of

London went lyrical "For anyone to score so freely on a dry and cracking surface was a prize-winning feat; for one to do so while wickets tumbled all around was the mark of a champion." India won the toss and batted first, abjectly it must be said, to be all out for 214. Most of the batsmen got into their 20s, including Tendulkar, but few progressed to anything substantial.

Javagal Srinath served notice of his batting potential with a knock of 52 and with young seamer Paras Mhambrey (28), added 53 runs for the ninth wicket which allowed India to creep past the 200-run mark. England batted positively against a quality new ball attack of Srinath and Venkatesh Prasad to secure a lead of 99 for themselves. It seemed a lead of immense proportion. India lost wickets quickly and when Azharuddin exposed his leg stump to be bowled by Allan Mullally, India had slipped to 36 for four.

Tendulkar, came to the crease at the fall of second wicket with only 17 on the board. England's pace attack was more than decent - Dominic Cork was still seen as an Ian Botham in the making, Chris Lewis' gifts were never in doubt though his mental frame was still a factor and Allan Mullally and Ronnie Irani had served much attention in county cricket.

Tendulkar's first boundary was off a steer to third man. He seemed set to bide his time and score off the bad balls. The state of the wicket dictated a cautious approach what with the ball swinging and dipping in helpful conditions and the Indian innings in complete disarray. Tendulkar went to the other extreme - watchful defence was interspersed with cracking strokeplay. Irani's arrival at the bowling crease was a moment of rare opportunity and Tendulkar on-drove, smashed past the covers and then pulled a four to end a productive over. In Irani's next over, Tendulkar repeated the dose with a cover boundary and a pulled four.

Tendulkar's pace didn't slacken even after debutant Sunil Joshi became the fifth batsman to be out for 68 and he was soon past his half century. Then in the company of Sanjay Manjrekar, he ensured India wasn't going to lose by an innings anyway. Tendulkar was in his 70s, in the team total of 127 when Manjraker failed to avoid a Lewis bouncer.

England, aware of the quality of Indian seamers and the fact they would be batting last on a deteriorating pitch, were beginning to lose their cool. Their fans were starved of wins in the recent past and with Pakistan due to tour in the second half of the summer, they needed to gain the maximum from the series against India, in the favourable conditions of early summer. Tendulkar was beginning to get under their skin because of the control, power and supreme authority he was displaying in the middle.

The visible sign of it all appeared when Lewis made a ball climb past the outside edge of Tendulkar's bat and everyone blasted a high decibel appeal at the umpire. Tendulkar, on 76 at this stage, suggested the ball had gone past his upper arm. It seemed to bring out in the open all the frustration of England captain Mike Atherton. He finger-wagged at the batsman, suggesting Tendulkar had no business to give his opinion to the umpire. It got ugly to the point where umpire David Shepherd had to step in and ask the England captain to watch his step - and his mouth. Indeed, Atherton was lucky to get away with just a reprimand from match referee Cammie Smith at the tea interval.

Tendulkar duly reached his hundred after tea, saw Anil Kumble and Javagal Srinath depart before the 200 was up and was the ninth batsman out, mishooking a catch to midwicket. His 122 had spanned 263 minutes and 177 balls and included a high percentage of boundary hits - 19 fours and a six in all. The shot for maximum hit - against the left-arm spin of Min Patel - actually brought him his hundred. The rest of the batsmen contributed only 97 runs between

them, including 14 extras. His innings was worth a memory of a lifetime. The funny thing was, so dominating did Tendulkar appear at the crease that one just wasn't aware India was losing wickets all the time. So mesmerising, it seemed he was good enough to bat from both ends - which he actually did on occasions - and those who watched were cast in the belief he somehow would remain in the middle as long as he pleased. Men with decades of experience of reporting in international cricket were already waging bets on Tendulkar's double hundred in the press box. This when Tendulkar had just crossed his hundred and was left with only a couple of wickets to carry on with his demolition. Rarely does one a domination so complete, an authority which mocks at any challenge.

The innings at Edgbaston was to bring far-reaching changes in Tendulkar's cricketing career. He was appointed captain - at 24 - as soon as India finished the tour of Blighty with a 1-0 Test scoreline against it. Tendulkar had a couple of Test hundreds in the series and despite the sensational debuts of Sourav Ganguly and Rahul Dravid, or for that matter the outstanding pace combination which Karnataka team-mates Srinath and Venkatesh Prasad worked between themselves in Tests, exuded a superior lustre of his own.

He took the team to Toronto for a five-match India-Pak series - a sham tourney at best of times - and defeated Mark Taylor's men in a one-off Test at Ferozeshah Kotla in New Delhi to suggest captaincy was his for keeps - or till he gets bored with it and chucks it away. He also defeated Hansie Cronje's men 2-1 in a three-Test series, a series which caused much bitterness and heart-burn among the Proteas who were not prepared to accept a loss in the Test arena. South Africa, after their readmission to international cricket in the early 90s, were keen to make up for their banishment of over 22 years in double quick time and had little patience and understanding when it came to defeats. They were keen to let the world know they stood in a different league even

after such a prolonged absence and wanted to whip up a nationalistic fervour among fans back home. After losing out on international attention, they wanted to be seen as winners and grow the domestic audience for cricket.

Things started to go wrong for Tendulkar from this stage onwards. He was to take an Indian team on two daunting tours of South Africa and West Indies in the first half of 1997 and the year's schedule also included a visit to Sri Lanka, freshly crowned one-day champions in world cricket and keen to be one-up on their sub-continent's cricketing super power neighbours - India and Pakistan. Tendulkar surely couldn't have had any inkling of what lay in store for him and his team and being aware he was more than a match for most of his opposition in world cricket, presumed the same degree of competence from his young team. He also had not bargained for the dark, sulking disposition of Mohammad Azharuddin who was smarting at the loss of captaincy which he had kept for the first six years of the 90s.

Thus Tendulkar was a picture of confidence when India took on the Proteas at Kingsmead, Durban on December 26, 1996 - usually known as the Boxing Day Test in the cricket summer of Australia. The small Indian media contingent on the tour were as keyed up for the revenge series as were fans in their millions back home. Rajan Bala, now a wizened old cricket writer with decades of experience behind him, thought India should look to hold the Proteas to a draw in the Test series. "Nothing would infuriate them more - for they want revenge and would settle for nothing less than a comprehensive win." He even said so to Tendulkar, on the eve of the match, in the middle of the picturesque Kingsmead ground. Tendulkar, casting a look back at the square in the middle - undistinguishable from the rest of the ground so green was it - replied with a rather confronting air "No, we would look to win the series." He didn't know or probably didn't realise India's away-win

record could be counted on his finger tips. A look at the pitch in Durban could have made anyone realise so. South Africa batted first and India got them out for 250 odd but before cheers could be heard in the Indian dressing room, home coach Bob Woolmer was busy telling the media, this was the highest his team had managed on this pitch for a few Tests now. It should have made the alarm bells ring in Indian quarters - it didn't and so the whole team was shot out for just 66 runs. Allan Donald was well nigh unplayable and Tendulkar was himself bowled through the gate. "A ball from hell," was a unanimous opinion. Tendulkar, to this day, doesn't believe Donald "bowled" that delivery. "I think more than him, it was the pitch which made it come from nowhere to hit the stumps." India were all out for 100 in the second innings and the Proteas couldn't have started their journey of revenge on a more forceful note.

The second Test was scheduled at Newlands in Cape Town. There was a huge build up for the game at the venue. The home media was busy dipping their pen in the ink of patriotic frenzy and the home audience was baying for the Indians blood. The backdrop of the picturesque Table Mountain appeared a sight of divine presence.

South Africa elected to bat on what appeared a benign pitch. It's progress was smooth and unhindered, helped no doubt by two dropped chances off Gary Kirsten who is not the kind of batsman to miss out on generosity. He was missed by Mohammad Azharuddin in the slips and Anil Kumble in the gully before he had entered double figures. His fourth hundred in Test cricket was the highlight of the day's play, as was his 114 run third wicket stand with Daryll Cullinan who was elegance personified in hitting a classy 77 runs. The Indian bowlers seemed to lose heart early and whenever Srinath and Prasad were out of the firing line, the rest were clueless to match the relentless South African march. The next day, Brian McMillan and Lance Klusener piled on the misery with centuries against their name and

South Africa at 529 for seven wickets declared had assumed the heights everyone had expected of them. More so when India slid to 3/29 by close. Tendulkar came out to quietly play the remaining four deliveries before the close of play.

When Sourav Ganguly left Tendulkar's company first thing in the morning and Venkat Sai Laxman departed at 58 for five to Shaun Pollock, India were again looking down the barrell it seemed. Tendulkar was now joined by his former skipper, Azhar and by all accounts the former wanted a more responsible approach from his senior this time. It implied less given to impulse and hectic strokeplay and more towards building a tattered innings.

There were early signs that the script would not be followed as the young skipper had ordained. Azhar, one of the more outstanding onside players the game has produced, relished the prospect of Lance Klusener's slanted deliveries on his pads and couldn't help but flick them profitably in the arc between midwicket and fine leg. Tendulkar, though looking more solid, was not losing any opportunities either against other South African bowlers. Both of them of course were helped by attacking field placements but still given the plight of the team, it was a brave option they had opted for.

The second session of the day though saw a partnership of rare magnificence unfold in front of a packed audience. It was a Saturday and the fans had converged at Newlands in the hope of a quick demolition by their heroes. The message was clear straightaway when Azhar picked up three fours in Klusener's initial offering and followed it up with two more in the bowler's next over. Tendulkar's duel with Allan Donald at the other end was a classic confrontation. Donald steamed in to bowl with his customary hostility, using his vast experience and the supposed upperhand of the first Test to test the mettle of the young champion. Tendulkar was presenting the full face of the blade mostly, which grew broader and broader as the minutes ticked by. A punched drive past mid-off off Donald, followed by one executed in the extra cover region was too good to be true. The South Africans had no inkling the carpet would be pulled from under their feet so quickly. They stood rooted to their spot as fours flowed in all directions.

When Azharuddin was dismissed for 115 from just 110 balls with 19 fours and a six at 280 for six, the two had added 222 runs for the sixth wicket in just 40 overs. It was a signal for Tendulkar to grow more hectic in his strokeplay. The South Africans, clueless and utterly subjugated to this mastery from the little champion, start plugging away at the other end with profit. Nayan Mongia was leg before to Adams for five and Kumble became Donald's second victim of the innings. Tendulkar seemed mildly respectful to Brian McMillan's crafty change of pace and line but overall his mastery was a sight to behold. When he became the last batsman to be dismissed for 169 from six and a half hours of batting, inclusive of 26 fours, it took everyone by surprise. It was a firm pull he had executed off McMillan and the ball seemed to have comfortably cleared Adam Bacher at square leg before the fielder jumped in the air and somehow plucked the chance out of thin air.

India was all out for 359 and the resurgence seemed to have rubbed on to the rest of his team as from the 12 remaining overs of the day, the hosts slid to 24 for two, losing Kirsten and Bacher for noughts. That they progressed to 256 for six declared on the fourth day and finally got India out of the way for 144 on the final day for a comfortable win in no way detracted from the big story of the match and it was Tendulkar's masterly innings and his stand with Azharuddin. It would remain one of the most memorable moments of Test cricket ever played in the history of the game.

Tendulkar didn't have a satisfying first stint as captain. He lost key players in key series, critics questioned his form though the weight of his runs should have been enough to silence them. What was said to be the worst year of his international cricket, was still worth over a thousand Test and one-day runs. May be, the legions of his fans had a genuine reason to feel disappointed since the flamboyance of his early years seemed to have deserted him at the time. He seemed to be more cautious and worn down by the demands of captaincy. A particularly distressing period was the Barbados Test of 1997 against the West Indies. India failed to make 120 runs to win the Test. It marked a real low in the young master's life. One would never forget the next morning after the match with downcast Indians at the airport trying to catch a plane to Antigua where the next Test was scheduled. Nobody dared to come close to him, not coach nor the senior members of the side.

Tendulkar's captaincy trauma only turned more and more painful as days - and matches - went by. He had to leave and it happened before the year 1997 was out. The pendulum had swung back astonishingly, once again, in favour of Azharuddin. Wiseheads in cricket suggest the sacking of a captain regularly is never a good idea to build a fine team. More so if the players are assured of their berths in the team and find it difficult to live down the humiliation of losing top spot. It happened to Azhar when he was deprived of his long-held post in 1996. He sulked and was uncooperative. Would the same thing happen to Tendulkar now?

The concern was genuine. But astonishingly, quite remarkably for which he has not been given enough credit, Tendulkar made the year 1998 his best of all. India won nine one-day finals that year and Tendulkar played a major role in practically everyone of them. He scored nearly 2000 one-day runs, quite unprecedented and it astounded the cricketing world. He also produced an innings of rare quality and charm against the touring, marauding Australians at the Chinnaswamy stadium in Chennai, his favourite hunting ground. The Australians toured India in

1998 for a three-Test series and Mark Taylor's men were on a mission. Australia were on a high at this stage of their cricketing history. They had beaten West Indies in the Caribbean a few years ago and were beginning to be seen as the best team on the planet. Shane Warne exercised a particularly high influence in their climb to the top. He was the world's best leg-spinner, rated by most already as the best of all-time, and he could trouble even the Pakistanis who, being a team from the sub-continent, were said to be particularly adept in playing spin bowling. Taylor was categorical in his desire to beat India in India. He believed if you are the best, you should be able to prevail in all and any conditions and the sub-continent was his final challenge, the final frontier if you may. He had been able to beat Pakistan in Pakistan and even though the team lost the 1996 World Cup final to Sri Lanka in Lahore, it had done enough to fancy its chances in taxing Indian conditions.

Tendulkar, like everyone else, was keyed up himself to do well in the series. An early sparring round involved a match between reigning Ranji Trophy champions Mumbai and the visiting Australians. The interest in the match was more than you see in a few Test matches these days. Everyone was busy tuning in to the radio - a few privileged were already hooked on to the internet - and newspapers were being called to find out the latest score. Mumbai batted first and Tendulkar, in a little matter of four and a half hours had hit a double hundred. Tendulkar faced just 192 balls for his double hundred which included 25 fours and two sixes. Shane Warne went without a wicket and conceded 111 runs from just 16 overs. It was heady stuff and the stage for anexciting Test series.

When the first Test began in Chennai, everyone was keen to know whether Warne had deliberately allowed himself to be thrashed so as to breed a sense of complacency among the Indian batsmen. Chennai, weatherwise, is the most taxing of all Indian Test venues. There are three kinds of weather seen at this venue year long - hot, hot and hotter! This, accompanied by a certain humidity because of the presence of the sea makes it a particularly draining experience for the cricketers. The strip in the middle is very unIndian-like and fast bowlers, at least in the last two decades, have always been helped by a generous bounce from it. It has also produced some epic dramas in the past - like the tied Test of 1986, a match made no less famous by a double hundred of extreme courage and grittiness from Dean Jones.

India won the toss and as it happens in this part of the world, promptly elected to bat first. Winning the toss in the sub-continent is always a bonus. Because if you are batting last, you could be sure the loose top would almost surely have disappeared. The ball would kick or keep low and do all kinds of funny things. So India began well by calling correctly and then when the openers, Navjot Singh Sidhu and Nayan Mongia put on over 100 runs for the first wicket, round one had surely gone in favour of the home team.

The two openers, indeed, batted for over three hours together. But then, in a matter of half an hour, India lost three wickets including the scalp of Tendulkar. Mongia left to a catch by Ian Healy behind the stumps of Kasprowicz and Sidhu's propensity to get tired after a particularly long innings resulted in a run-out. Tendulkar arrived amidst a generous round of applause. He promptly hit a four before a mighty drive aimed at Shane Warne could only edge a sharp flying chance at first slip where Mark Taylor somehow clasped his hands together to send the little master packing. There was a deathly silence at the stadium and Warne could be forgiven in believing the world now lay at his feet. The sceptics had that I-told-you-so look on their face, stressing once again that Warne had reserved his best for the big matches and centre stage.

Warne was also to account for Mohammad Azharuddin on day one and as the hosts ended at 232 for five, it was clear with whom the honours of the day rested with. India were to be all out for 257 the next day, Warne, returning impressive figures of 4 for 85 from 35 long overs, but much of the visitors' advantage was lost with the way they batted. The Indian spinners spun a web around their uncertain feet and a close score of 193 for seven meant India was back in the game.

As so often happens in an Australian innings, the edifice of the innings was effected by the lower half of the batting. Ian Healy was the prime player in this restoration drama, batting on and on for his 90 runs for four hours and 20 minutes, intent on frustrating the Indian bowlers with high competence in defence and grinding tactics. He put on 96 runs for the ninth wicket with debutant Gavin Robertson who became the last batsman to be out for 57 at the total of 328. India had conceded a first innings lead of 71 runs which was invaluable under the circumstances. Not only had the visitors gone ahead from a hopeless position, they had done so by keeping the hosts on the field at least three hours longer than they had anticipated.

Much before the Australians had seized the initiative and progressed in the match thus far, as they had envisaged, Tendulkar had enveloped himself into a cover of isolation - a period of deep introspection. Anshuman Gaekwad, a former India Test opener marked for his courage against West Indies fast bowlers of the 80s, said looking at him he knew something special was due from the little genius in the second innings. Before he went on to bat the second time, Tendulkar is said to have uttered thus to Gaekwad: "Don't worry, I will get a big one this time around."

Sure, he had a perfect platform to carry on with his resolve to fix Warne. India had ended the third day, one down for 100 with Navjot Sidhu looking in resplendent form once again in his unbeaten 55. He departed early for 64 at 115 the next morning but Dravid was settling into his groove nicely when Tendulkar took guard for the second time in the match. Warne was operating at this point and it only heightened the sense of drama. Tendulkar decided early to hit Warne against the spin, a particularly dangerous ploy since the blond leg spinner usually pitches outside the leg-stump in the rough, doesn't flight much and curiously is still able to derive prodigious spin. Sure, he gets good protection from his captain on the offside but for a batsman, willing to take his chances on the onside, there are runs aplenty to be had.

The belligerence from Tendulkar was astonishing as he struck 155 from just 191 balls, including four sixes and 14 fours and provided a supersonic momentum to the innings. In all 318 runs were scored for the loss of three more wickets from just 73 overs. India declared at 418 for four and set Australia a target of 348 from a minimum of 105 overs. The visitors, devastated by the surprising turnaround in the game, were tottering at 31 for three from the remaining 15 overs of the day.

This was Tendulkar's third Test century in seven appearances against Australia. The power he imparted to his strokes was breathtaking and his placement was impeccable. He reserved his special attention for Warne, repeatedly coming down the track and hitting him against the spin in the vacant onside field and on a few occasions even managed straight sixes over the bowler's heads. He reached his half century from just 64 balls and hundred off another 63, a span in which he hit three sixes.

Tendulkar, a man inspired by the occasion and the stature of his opponents, took batting to a rarefied zone on the day. Inside the stadium, it was hot, humid and oppressive. The Aussies, famous for their relentless attack and ability to build up pressure, were unable to throw up any answer to Tendulkar's magic. Taylor saw his ambitious plans for India blown up in the course of a single afternoon. Still, he showed enough to demonstrate of his reputation as an outstanding leader of modern times. He never stopped attacking the Indians - indeed the Australians are known to have a tradition of attacking at all times and backed his premier bowler - Shane Warne. He showed the utmost confidence in Warne and kept giving him an attacking field even when he was hit around the park. There was no protection in the deep on either side of the wicket for Warne - not at midwicket nor at sweeper covers. Warne claimed only Rahul Dravid and conceded 122 runs from 30 expensive overs.

Australia, set on the back foot by the loss of three wickets on the penultimate evening, went down tamely the next day for 168, with Anil Kumble leading a pack of spinners on a worn out track. India were winners by 179 runs and the course of the series was decisively shifted in favour of India from then on. It was the reconfirmation of Tendulkar's sway over the Australians and Warne in particular. The bowler, once back home, confessed he still had nightmares about Tendulkar coming down the track and hitting him over his head. Importantly, the Australian team had one more opportunity of agreeing with what their cricketing icon Don Bradman had said a couple of years ago - that the young Indian master comes closest to him on the matter of style and strokeplay.

Chennai was again the venue of Tendulkar's next epic stance. The circumstances of this match couldn't have come in a more volatile situation. India had just returned from New Zealand where they had suffered a 1-0 series loss in 1999. The senior players were most distressed by the endless grind of cricket which their administrators had subjected them to, and in a famous meeting among themselves in New Zealand, sought to convey to their bosses back home that they would rather pull out than play another gruelling series. The bone of contention was the hurry with which India had agreed to host arch-rivals Pakistan at home for a three-Test series. Players were not only tired, they were also

afraid of playing against a team they usually ended up losing to. They felt in no condition to take on the might of the Pakistanis and worried about the backlash which might follow from the cricket-mad home audience and administrators. They were also extremely keen to retain their berths for the World Cup scheduled in England that summer.

The first day of the Chennai Test though was enough to lift their spirits. Pakistan wasted the advantage of batting first and were all out for 238, at least 60 short of a potential 300-plus total. In the previous decade 15 of the 16 Tests between the two sides had been drawn so here appeared an opportunity for India to break the deadlock. Kumble, playing his 50th Test but first against Pakistan, took the day's honours with six for 70. He was well nigh unplayable with his high bounce and nagging length though it must be said the Pakistani batsmen were guilty of not applying themselves as required. In the remaining eight overs of the day, the Indian openers batted with such flourish that as many as 48 runs were up on the board. debutant left-hander Sadgopan Ramesh seemed nerveless in compiling 30 runs off 22 balls.

On the second day, India suffered a series of jolts and finished only 16 runs in front - negligible, when one considers they had the Pakistanis on the mat on the first day and that they had to bat last on this wicket. Only Sourav Ganguly and Rahul Dravid were the two batsmen to make half centuries. Surprisingly, it was the visiting spinners who inflicted the maximum damage and took eight Indian wickets. Off-spinner Saqlain Mushtaq almost bowled without a break for his 34 overs to take a five-wicket haul. Shahid Afridi, with his round-arm leg-breaks which never turned, chipped in with three wickets.

Tendulkar lasted just three balls before he dashed down the wicket to Saqlain, looking to hoick him towards the midwicket boundary. Only, he misjudged the extent of turn and bounce on the delivery and a leading edge went straight into the hands of Salim Malik in the point region.

Back in the dressing room, Ashok Malhotra, a national selector, said he had never seen Tendulkar so downcast and angry with himself. He seemed beside himself, working himself into a rage and apparently speaking to himself in a fit. "I have lost it, I have lost my concentration." Malhotra later said after seeing Tendulkar in that mood, he was almost certain the little master would redeem himself with a big knock in the second innings.

But before Tendulkar could bring himself to do it, there was this little matter of Pakistan's second innings. Pakistan lost Saeed Anwar on the second evening but the next morning, Shahid Afridi and Inzamam ul Haq got into top gear straightaway. Not till Tendulkar bowled one of his mystery balls and claimed Haq, caught at forward short leg, was there any success to be had for the Indians. Still, 121 runs came in the opening two hours and the pendulum of the game was decidedly shifting in Pakistan's favour.

After lunch, Tendulkar struck again when he claimed Yousuf Youhana with a big leg break. But Pakistan continued to press on to the pedal through Afridi's belligerence. The youngster, only recently introduced to the Test eleven after proving himself in the one-day arena, went on to score 141 before Venkatesh Prasad, in an astonishing spell, took five wickets in 18 balls. Pakistan were finally all out for 286, leaving India 271 to win the Test and go one-up in the series.

It was a tall order in the fourth innings against a charged up visiting side. More so when India lost both its openers, Ramesh and Laxman, with only six on the board. Tendulkar was tentative to start with and survived a strong shout for leg before by Waqar Younis before surviving the day in the company of Rahul Dravid. India 40 for two at close, needed 231 on the final day. India couldn't have had a worse start to their chase on the final morning. Dravid survived a good shout from Akram but wasn't good enough to cover up an angled away swinger from the legendary Pakistan fast bowler which clipped his off bail. Saqlain, at the other end, was keeping Tendulkar quiet and caused him to mistime his strokes. Saqlain earned a positive response to have Azhar out leg before who played forward without offering a shot. Ganguly was given out in a bizzarre fashion - and wrongly - when he cut Saqlain on to the shin of one of the silly point fielders and it hit the ground before Moin picked up the chance on the rebound. New Zealand's Steve Dunne consulted his partner, India's V.K. Ramasway, to know whether Moin had picked up the chance neatly or not, without realising the ball had already been grounded.

Progress in the morning session was slow as India pushed and prodded for only 46 runs in two hours. Indeed, by the time the tea break was taken, India had advanced their score by only 107 runs in four hours. India though were not to lose a single wicket in the afternoon session as Tendulkar and wicketkeeper Nayan Mongia dug their heels in. At one stage, 90 minutes went by without a boundary. Saqlain was proving a miserly influence on the Indian innings with only 31 runs from 19 overs.

Tendulkar survived a vociferous appeal from Saqlain after the tea break. He had hardly hit a ball in the air in the first four hours. He now ventured out to hit Saqlain for four fours in the next over - and also survive a stumping chance when a surprised Moin Khan failed to gather the ball. After giving away 25 runs in three overs, Saqlain was taken out of the attack.

As Tendulkar's innings went into overdrive in the final session, it was also a signal of extreme distress for him. Everytime he went forward, pain shot through his back to

his lower half and he was jolted everytime he made a forward motion. Sensing his physical discomfort, the Pakistani bowlers were intent on drawing him forward. Looking at Tendulkar, one could see he was in no position to carry on batting but somehow he pulled along, even twice driving Akram down the ground for four.

With India now closing in on Pakistan's target, the two batsmen were seen consulting each other more often in the middle. The stand grew and was worth 136 runs when Mongia, inexplicably, went to hit Akram over the top and only succeeded in giving a catch to Waqar Younis at mid-on. New man Sunil Joshi now got four leg byes to third man and even hit Saqlain for a straight six.

Tendulkar was visibly very tired and suffered from spasms in the back. He seemed keen to finish the game in a hurry and smashed Saqlain straight into the sightscreen for a four and then pulled him for another boundary to square leg. But then, trying to loft the next ball over the bowler's head, he holed out to Akram at deep mid off. India now needed only 17 runs but Pakistan were back in the picture. Tendulkar had batted heroically for 405 minutes and hit 18 fours from 378 deliveries for his valiant 136 runs.

Kumble survived a leg before shout but then fell in a similar manner to Akram. From the other end, Joshi offered a catch back to Saqlain. Now the last pair needed 15 to win. Prasad survived a torrid over from Saqlain but not Srinath in the next and Pakistan were winners by 12 runs.

As Tendulkar lay on the physio's bench, match referee Cammie Smith announced at the presentation ceremony that it was he, and not Afridi and Saqlain who finished with match figures of 10 for 187, who was his man of the match. Tendulkar was in no position to collect the award but he would have bargained it with anything else to win the match for his country. He says now: "In my heart and heart I know,

Pakistan had given it up," he pauses to think, then repeats "They had given it up." Pakistan's skipper Wasim Akram was magnanimous in defeat. "I have long said that Tendulkar is the best batsman in the world and today we saw one of the best innings I have ever seen played."

Tendulkar's close associates and doctors who subsequently attended to his back injury, vouch that he took that defeat to heart. It was a long, long time before he overcame the trauma of that reverse in Chennai. Even now, a mention of that match makes his visage a grim one.

That series against Pakistan also marked Tendulkar's first decade in international cricket. By a strange coincidence, his first Test, 10 years back, was also against Pakistan. Ironically, the two nations had no Test exchanges in between these two series. His career was now in the high water of success and more success, records and more records. He was already past 20 Test hundreds in Tests and in one-dayers, his position was peerless. It appeared soon very few peaks would now be left for him to conquer.

A disturbing trough at this stage was his back injury. His propensity to hit pulls and hooks off just short of a length balls appeared to have placed unreasonable demands on his back. He would swivel on his backfoot and seek to punish these deliveries when, sometimes, still appearing cramped in his movement. Without the right balance of feet and space for rotation, his back over the years had sustained severe stress. It finally put him into medical supervision. His desire to get back to his prime fitness made him submit to the required levels of sacrifice, including a check on his body weight as well as the mandatory sleep on a hard board.

Soon he was back to his favourite passion of making runs. He lost his father during the 1999 World Cup in England where India qualified for the super six stage but suffered some unpalatable defeats, including one against Zimbabwe in the league round which threw their campaign out of gear. Tendulkar missed a couple of matches and even though he made a hundred on return, India could make little headway in the premier competition of the world.

But India's below par performance during the 1999 World Cup made Indian cricket officialdom once again look for a scapegoat and the selectors looked at Tendulkar in askance one more time. The musical chair of captaincy between Tendulkar and Azharuddin, it appeared, would go on and on. Only Tendulkar, one is given to believe, was willing to accept the captaincy only if the subversive influence of Azhar was not cast on his team. There is little to dispute this line of opinion, backed by circumstantial evidence since Azhar was neither picked in the home series against New Zealand nor was taken to Australia for a three-Test series.

India was practically mauled by Steve Waugh's men in the Australian summer of 1999-2000 and when Hansie Cronje managed to thrash the Indians at home 2-0, India's magic run even at home had finally come to an end. An Indian team had not lost a series at home for over a dozen years before Cronje broke that spell. Azharuddin was brought back into the side in the Bangalore Test after India were thumped from all quarters. It was a development which influenced Tendulkar to relinquish captaincy once again.

Sourav Ganguly was now the Indian captain and as with Azhar, Tendulkar was whole-hearted in his commitment to him and to the team. India did well enough to reach the finals of the ICC mini world cup in Nairobi and later in Sharjah and when the Zimbabweans toured in the winter of 2000, Tendulkar helped himself to a century and a double century in two Tests. It was now the turn of Waugh's men to take up for the unfinished task of their predecessors, Mark Taylor and his army, but in the three-Test series, they were beaten yet again. Tendulkar was successful but the spotlight was firmly fixed on VVS Laxman and Harbhajan

"Turbanator" Singh. Tendulkar didn't get a hundred against Zimbabwe in an away tour and then missed the three-Test series against Sri Lanka because of a toe injury. He was declared fit for the gruelling series against South Africa in the closing months of 2001 and was keen to check out his form and the state of his injury. He did manage a hundred in the very first one-day international but then had to go back to his South African physio to have an additional cushion inserted in his shoes. Apparently, being out of action for so long and now standing on the field for six hours at a stretch, he found the specially fitted shoes were still not good enough to give his sore feet the proper support.

The first Test of the series was scheduled at Bloemfontein, home of Afrikaan-speaking people of South Africa and better still, known as the place where Hansie Cronje grew up and played most of his cricket. The build up for the match was lukewarm, more so since the rugby season of South Africa was in full swing.

South Africa won the toss and elected to field against the Indians, looking to exploit the weakness of the visitors against the rising ball on a fresh wicket. They were not off the mark as India began to lose wickets at an alarming rate.

India in the last season had discovered an opener in Shiv Sunder Das but his partner's slot was still vacant. Rahul Dravid, a reluctant opener, was asked to step in and help the team's cause. He wasn't much of a help though as he lasted just 15 deliveries before falling to Shaun Pollock in the slips. VVS Laxman played some gorgeous strokes and raced to 32 from 30 balls but the devil-may-care batsmanship wasn't going to last for long. Das himself potted around for 55 minutes before falling to Nantie Hayward for nine. When captain Ganguly fell to Kallis for 14, India were 4 down for 68 in just 20 overs.

Tendulkar, who had been at the crease for half an hour or so at this stage, realised he was running out of partners. The next man to join him was Virender Sehwag who was playing in his first Test. after that, wicketkeeper Deep Dasgupta, was also making his debut. Anil Kumble, Javagal Srinath, Zaheer Khan and Ashish Nehra struggled to succeed with the bat on a benign pitch and were unlikely to hold their ends up now against a lively attack on fire.

Tendulkar cut lose and how. Buoyed by their success, the South African pacemen kept digging the ball in, rising it above the rib cage and making sure the little master didn't get many deliveries to drive on the up. They bowled to him short and wide on the off-stump, trying to keep him pinned at one end and frustrating him to his doom. Tendulkar wasted little time in adjusting to the demands of the situation. He now started to employ the slash with good effect. Balls started zooming over the slips head with alarming regularity. There was no third man and the slices were hitting the hoardings as if some canon was finding its target. The shots were disappearing in the country zone in a flash. At one stage, he had hit eight fours from 18 balls as India recovered to be 123 for four at lunch.

Tendulkar turned his attention to the pacey but predictable Makhaya Ntini after lunch and the fast bowler's first four overs cost 36 runs. The hour after lunch, if anything, saw more furious strokeplay and 63 runs were realised. Tendulkar moved closer to his hundred and crossed the landmark of 7,000 Test runs. His 26th century came soon enough, putting him on par with Steve Waugh and making him fourth in the all-time list of Test century-makers.

As Sehwag grew emboldened in his idol's company, no less than 220 runs were realised for the fifth wicket which lifted India to 288 for five. Tendulkar at this stage fell to Ntini, going for yet another attacking stroke and scooping it up for Neil McKenzie to run-in from the square leg boundary and accept the chance. His 155 came off just 184 deliveries and had the high percentage of 23 fours and a six. The impression he had rubbed on his younger partner was not going to be lost in a hurry and Sehwag scooped a debut century for himself as India finished the day at 372 for 7. A position of utter hopelessness transformed by the brilliance and inspiration of a single individual.

This innings by Tendulkar must be viewed for its sheer innovation and daring. One doesn't often see a Test batsman slash so regularly and so deliberately against a high quality attack when everything was stacked against his team. He was doing so with pin-point accuracy, measuring the distance and height of the slip fielders so it should elude them perfectly. When a third man was finally placed, he started cutting it wide and over the gully fielder's head, rendering such a move utterly useless.

India were to lose the Test nevertheless but the gloss stayed firmly on Tendulkar's work of art. The master, a picture of modesty, was willing to underplay it and allow centrestage to young Virender Sehwag. If anything, it only lent a well-rounded look to Tendulkar's knock.

O N E   D A Y   C A R E E R

The records show that Tendulkar has 31 one-day hundreds from 278 innings, a shade under one in every nine outings. His 11 thousand plus runs are nearly two thousand runs more than the next best; his 105 wickets and 93 catches suggest he is not about runs alone. For a man whose first century took 79 long matches in coming, Tendulkar has shown surprising urgency in piling up the evidence of runs to lay claim to be the best in the one-day business, as he is in Tests.

When you judge a batsman to be the best in his field, more than runs go into deciding this sweeping opinion. Not only are his runs useful, his presence also acts in uplifting the standards of men playing around him. Style and domination also matters as does the number of wins he inspires for the colours he represents. Tendulkar rates true on most of these counts. If he is not there in the end in a particularly frenetic run-chase of a one-day contest, it is only because he is an opener and acts more as a layer of base rather than a provider of the finishing touches. In that sense, he is more like a ball-maker on a football field and not a climactic striker.

Tendulkar's one-day career, indeed reputation, rests solely on his body of work as an opener. If one-day cricket is mostly about statistics, this one is damning conclusive: He has opened in 193 of his 278 innings and scored 8743 of his 11069 runs at 49.12 with an unbeaten 186 against New Zealand in Hyderabad as his best. Thirty of his 31 hundreds have come at this position, the sole exception being the knock of 140 which he essayed against Kenya at Bristol during the 1999 World Cup, an innings of special significance because he had just returned from India after attending his father's funeral, the man with whom Tendulkar shared the deepest of all bonds.

Tendulkar became an opener out of choice rather than one groomed for the role by his seniors. He had already been in

international cricket for five seasons and struck five Test hundreds when his first one in limited overs arrived against Australia at the Premadasa Stadium in Sri Lanka in the 1994-95 Singer Cup. He struck 110 from 130 balls and the memory of that day seems to hold him in good stead whenever he turns out against the men with the baggy greens; a record of 1626 runs from 33 matches at 49. 27 average with six hundreds is a testimony to it.

As said, Tendulkar was hardly in the scheme of things of his seniors when he pleaded to be given a chance to open the innings at Auckland, during the second one-day international of a short tour of a Test and four limited overs game. The tour was notable because the solitary Test was the final one, number 131, in the long career of a certain Kapil Dev. It was also the tour where in a moment of uncommon openness, Venkata Rao, the manager of the Indian team, suggested at least six members of the Indian team were hobnobing with men of dubious credentials. The board was quick to rubbish the claim, suggesting he must have been speaking out of his mind or was under the influence of liquor. Rao then denied having ever spoken to the press!

India had a bad start to the one-day series. They lost the first one at Napier by 28 runs, made remarkable by the hat-trick which Danny Morrison effected through his reverse swing, clean bowling Kapil Dev, Salil Ankola and Nayan Mongia. Tendulkar, coming in at number five, made 15 from 19 balls before becoming Dion Nash's scalp. India needed to win at Auckland to keep their heads above water in the series.

The lead-up to the Auckland game was hardly encouraging. Navjot Singh Sidhu, who was impressive in the first game with a 34 from 42 deliveries, pulled out because of a neck strain and was replaced by a bowler - off-spinner Rajesh Chauhan. This left India with a batsman short. To

compound matters, the pitch at Auckland was being looked at suspiciously: It was at this track where a one-day international between New Zealand and Pakistan had earlier ended in a tie.

Still, New Zealand captain Ken Rutherford elected to bat on winning the toss. It turned out to be a bad choice as in no time at all, the hosts had slipped to 34 for five. Kapil Dev, along with young hopes Salil Ankola and Javagal Srinath, were virtually unplayable on a pitch which afforded sideways movement. The ball was swinging and even stopping a bit. But the conditions eased a bit thereafter and it was so slow the batsmen had trouble getting it off the square. Chris Harris played well for his 50 off 72 balls but New Zealand still only managed 142.

Since the pitch was slow, the Indians reckoned they must make the best use of the first 15 overs when the field restriction was in force when a harder ball with faster bowlers were in action. Also, India didn't want to bring the match to a stage where a longish tail would be asked to indulge in a operation. Tendulkar, in a rare departure from his usual reticent self, now pleaded to be sent at the top of the order. Reminiscences Tendulkar: "I requested to be sent in as an opener. I always fancied my chances of batting with the field restrictions being enforced in the first 15 overs. Fortunately, my plea was accepted."

As it turned out, the game was virtually over in the first 15 overs. Tendulkar smashed 82 off 49 balls with 15 fours and three sixes, most of them in front of the wicket. His power and style was captivating on the day: a pushed drive with the minimum of follow through was still whistling past the bowlers to the pickets; sixes were being hit over the bowler's head and ondrives and pulls came in torrents. A large number of his fours were sent crashing into the hoardings with one bounce. Morrison had been brought back to earth with a thud - he was still bowling at a reasonable clip,

around the 130kph mark, and was troubling batsmen at the other end. Tendulkar though was different. It came to a stage when the bowlers were just laughing in a sort of resigned submission. When he was caught by bowler Matt Horne in his follow through off a leading edge, the game was as good as over.

This was the 70th knock of his one-day career and it was only a matter of time before his maiden century would arrive, assured as he was of opening the innings from now on. He followed the knock at Auckland with substantial knocks in the two remaining one-dayers of the series: 63 at Basin Reserve in Wellington and 40 at Jade Stadium in Christchurch. His next innings in Sharjah against UAE took him past 2,000 one-day international runs and he followed it up with 73 against arch-rivals Pakistan. People who watched this innings would remember it long for the duel it showcased between Tendulkar and Wasim Akram. Tendulkar first crashed Wasim through the covers and then swung him over square leg for a six. Akram's response was to bowl a short quick delivery which, even on a slow Sharjah surface, climbed up steeply to leave a dent on Tendulkar's helmet.

Fittingly, some of Tendulkar's best knocks came during the year 1998 when he amassed 1894 runs from 33 innings at 65.31 with as many as nine hundreds. Four of them were against Australia: three, each a masterpiece in its own right. As if his batting exploits were not enough, he even took five wickets against them in a match to leave the Aussies utterly devastated. Each of these efforts deserve a detailed look for in it the essential Tendulkar is framed: focussed and uncomplicated; a cricketer who is at his best when the opponents are as good as the Australians.

The year of 1998 would largely be remembered in world cricket as the one in which Sachin Tendulkar almost single-handedly subdued the Australians in their ambitions on

many a field. First, Mark Taylor and his men wanted to win the Test series in India, a feat which no side had achieved in nearly a dozen years. Their hopes were not to be realised when the Indians won the three-Test series by a 2-1 margin and Tendulkar scored nearly 500 runs, including two big hundreds in the first and last Tests. The first one at Chennai was a classic in every sense of the word, no less because of the much-anticipated duel with Shane Warne which went out and out in favour of the Indian batsman.

Tendulkar would cross Australia's path again and again even in the one-day series. The first match at Kochi left Australia utterly frustrated. So hot were the conditions that Steve Waugh, by now the one-day captain of the side even though the reins in Tests were still in Taylor's hands (shades of recent times!), in a scathing reaction was to say later that someday, somebody was going to suffer a great deal in these conditions. He was to criticise the way the itinerary was planned with little gap in contests and matches scheduled at far-flung places.

Said Waugh: "I think it's just ridiculous playing in these conditions. If you were honest about it, you wouldn't even walk outside in this sort of heat and yet we're playing 100 overs of cricket in it. You just can't play sport in 45F, someone has got to look at the scheduling..."

Waugh wondered why the tournament, which also featured Zimbabwe, was scheduled in the day instead of being played in a day/night setting. He termed the entire package as "ridiculous."

The Jawaharlal Nehru Stadium in Kochi was crammed with 75,000 spectators and the heat and humidity was killing. India had a disastrous start on winning the toss, both Navjot Sidhu and Tendulkar contributing nine runs between them. Tendulkar survived only 11 balls for his eight runs before Ricky Ponting caught him inside the

circle off Michael Kasprowicz. India, astonishingly, still flourished as Mohammad Azharuddin and Ajay Jadeja put on 104 runs for the fourth wicket. Azhar had 82 from 91 balls with 10 fours while Jadeja was to remain unbeaten on 105 from 109 deliveries with 12 boundaries. Young Hrishikesh Kanitkar hit out boldly in the end as India crossed 300 - 309 for five to be exact.

Even though it was a massive total and the Australians were in the field for a good three and a half hours under a scorching sun, they were in no mood to give up without a fight. The positive vein of influence was evident in the approach of Mark Waugh and Adam Gilchrist as 102 runs came for the first wicket in just 11.2 overs. Debashis Mohanty, Orissa's honest trier who is a better bet on pitches which help him a bit, was carted for 51 runs in just five overs. Gilchrist smashed the ball all-around the park for a 37-ball half century

India's 300 plus target had suddenly begun to appear too small. The 200 of the innings was up in the 32nd over. Michael Bevan and Steve Waugh were proving a great influence in the middle overs and had put on 70 runs in just over 11 overs.

Tendulkar was already in the middle of his spell when he tasted his first success. It came in the form of Waugh's wicket who pushed back a chance for the bowler to accept when on 26. Darren Lehmann, one of the specialist one-day players, pushed hesitantly and fell leg before to Tendulkar who then had the prized wicket of Bevan, stumped by Mongia for 65. Bevan was beaten both in the air and off the pitch to set up a leg-side stumping by Mongia. India suddenly sensed a turnaround to their fortunes. Tendulkar was to account for Tom Moody and Damien Martyn as well and Australia crashed to 268 all out, leaving India winners by 41 runs. From a comforting 202 for three in the 32nd over, the last seven Australian wickets crashed for just 66

runs from 13-odd overs. Tendulkar's bewildering mix of spin and seam, yielded five wickets for only 32 runs in his 10 overs. He was unfathomable to most Australians, bowling leg-spin at the right-handers and off-spin to the left-handers.

The two sides then left for Sharjah to play a triangular series which also featured New Zealand. India had an inconsistent run till it came to the final league game of the tournament. Australia were already through to the finals and India's fate rested on mathematical equation. When the Australians made 284, India seemed as good as out of the tournament. They needed to make 255 to shut the door on the New Zealanders.

The Australian innings revolved around Bevan who scored his third century with trademark improvisations while Mark Waugh scored a typically elegant 81. Ricky Ponting and Darren Lehmann also played attractively and Australia had seemingly done enough to shut the door on the Indians. To compound matters further for the Indians, the target of 255 was revised to 237 after the match had been reduced to 46 overs following a dust-storm. They were 143 for four in 31 overs when the game was interrupted. To win the match, India needed 276 in 46 overs.

Tendulkar didn't start hammering the bowlers from the first ball. But the first aggressive shot was devastating enough: Tendulkar coming down the track to Michael Kasprowicz and seeing the bowler drop the ball short, swinging his bat in an arc with such robust power that the ball lay many a tier deep at the midwicket boundary. It was a savage stroke followed by another six off the same bowler in the same direction. Tendulkar had signalled his intention to take on the Australians.

A dust-storm in the middle of the innings almost disrupted the Indian plans. All of a sudden, the skyline in Sharjah was

filled with sandy dust and the game needed to be stopped. It appeared very messy and Tendulkar sported a dejected look as he walked away from the pitch with his partner VVS Laxman to the pavilion. India had just lost the wicket of Ajay Jadeja and before the innings could be stabilised, the dust-storm had caused another hiccup.

Tendulkar walked off from the field but didn't enter the dressing room. He kept sitting outside, with his helmet on, and waiting for the sky to clear. Millions in India, and worldwide, were glued to their television sets, unable to break themselves free even when the decent hour for sleep was long past. The weather did clear and Tendulkar was allowed to accomplish his unfinished job.

Sunil Gavaskar at the commentators' box had sensed something sensational. He kept saying Tendulkar would not rest at just India's qualification and indeed would try to win the game. Tendulkar did seem to go for the jugular. Instead of getting tired in the heat, his forearm seemed to impart more swing and power to his shots. Steve Waugh was the one to be mauled during this onslaught: the Australian captain conceding 65 runs in his nine overs.

With Tendulkar in this mood, India needed a batsman at the other end to bid for a win and not just qualify in this match. Laxman batted a shade too slowly for his 34 off 23 balls while Hrishikesh Kanitkar took 14 balls for his five runs. Tendulkar departed only after he had taken India to safe shores. His 143 from 131 balls till then being his highest in one-day cricket contained nine fours and five sixes. He departed at the end of the 43rd over, caught behind off Fleming, and at 242 for five, India had already qualified for the finals. For victory though, they needed to get 35 runs from the final three overs which was not to happen. Who knows if Tendulkar was around, India might have pulled off an improbable win.

But Tendulkar was very much around when India were asked to repeat the act against Australia in the finals, two days later. It was a special day for another reason: Tendulkar, on this day of 24th of April, was celebrating his 25th birthday. Australia had been much tormented by the long tour in this part of the world and equally keen to make the last official day of the trip a memorable one. Such was the build-up for the game that queues miles and miles long were forming outside the Sharjah Stadium long before the 2.30 p.m start. It wasn't an India-Pakistan game but Tendulkar had lit up a strange anticipation in this desert kingdom and the prospect of Warne against Tendulkar for one last time was too tempting to be ignored. Even the locals had never seen something like this in Sharjah before. A ticket inside the stadium was the most prized catch going in Sharjah that evening.

As a direct result of India's successful run-chase in the last league game, India's captain Mohammad Azharuddin chose to bat second on winning the toss in the finals. It was a strange, even bizarre decision, and in today's post match-fixing world would have invited more than just curious glances. His bowlers though vindicated the decision at least in the initial stage of the Australian innings when three wickets were gone with just 26 on the board. Venkatesh Prasad was extremely accurate while Ajit Agarkar bowled with his customary aggression to send back Mark Waugh (7), Ricky Ponting (1) and Tom Moody (1).

The Australian batting ran too deep to be derailed by the occasional collapses of the top order. Adam Gilchrist found Michael Bevan a willing ally and the two left-handers rode over the difficult period and yet did not allow the run-rate to drop. When Gilchrist was out for 45, Australia were 85 for four in the 21st over. Bevan, at the same personal score, left at 121 in the 26th over but Australia now had got their breath back. Captain Steve Waugh and Darren Lehmann put the Indian bowlers to the sword in putting on 103 runs

for the sixth wicket. Waugh made 70 off 71 balls while Lehmann was still more impressive at 70 off just 59 deliveries. The two batsmen ran hard between the wickets and hit only nine fours between them besides a hit each for the maximum. Australia finished at 272 for six in their 50 overs and it was now left to their bowlers to keep the domination going.

Sure, the target was not easy. India's batting lacked an allrounder and a batsman who could slay the bowling. The promotion of Nayan Mongia as a pinch-hitter at one-drop was a give away. The last four batsmen couldn't be relied upon much as Agarkar was just settling into the international arena and Anil Kumble, Prasad and Rahul Sanghvi lacked the ability to be of some dramatic use should the situation arise. India badly needed a stirring start from its openers, Sourav Ganguly and Tendulkar, who were already a formidable force at the top of the line-up.

Ganguly, on this day, just couldn't get his silken timing going. There is something about Sharjah that Ganguly struggles to make a decent total at this venue. It was no different in the finals as after pottering around for 42 balls for his 23 runs with two fours, Ganguly charged at Damien Fleming and presented Tom Moody with the easiest chance inside the circle.

Sensing the game would swiftly drift away from his team, Tendulkar indulged in some hectic hitting with Mongia. Mongia raised 28 for himself from 41 balls but Tendulkar hit through the line and found the gaps at will. So impressive was the recovery that the second wicket fell at 128 in the 25th over of the innings. India still needed close to 150 runs in the final 25 overs.

Tendulkar had worked out the batting details to such a nicety that he eased off the gas pedal. He understood there was no need to go for big shots, instead he shifted his focus

on staying at the wicket. While he milked the bowling, with the occasional flourish from one end, Mohammad Azharuddin made the most of a good platform to pick 58 runs for himself from 64 balls. The two put on 120 runs for the third wicket before Tendulkar was given out leg before to Kasprowicz for 134 from 131 balls with 12 fours and three sixes. His last three innings against the Australians had yielded 80, 143 and 134. In all, he had hit five hundreds in both forms of cricket against the Australians in a matter of a couple of months. India won in a canter in the end. Tendulkar was man of the match and the series, was gifted the keys of a new car, an award for hitting the most sixes (9) as well as a prize for scoring the fastest 50 - off 44 balls.

If the Australians were to believe that the Tendulkar nightmare was now over, it surfaced again, albeit in a different country and in a tournament where every international cricket team was represented. The 1998 Mini World Cup in Dhaka, the capital of Bangladesh, was the start of a biennial tournament, a brainchild of Jagmohan Dalmiya, then the International Cricket Council (ICC) chief. Dalmiya had earned his reputation for turning cricket into a money-spinning game and now he wanted money to be raised to be distributed for cricket's development at new posts. His mantra was cricket's globalisation. Even though the game's saner voices were not too convinced about the methods adopted for cricket's spread to newer outposts, there remains little doubt Dalmiya was responsible for filling up the ICC's empty coffers.

The tournament in Dhaka was hugely successful. There is tremendous enthusiasm for the game in Dhaka and venues are generally full whenever a big event takes place. The national team too had some notable gains in the 90s, not the least their promotion first to one-day and then, ultimately, to Test standards.

As it happened, Australia's first match of the tournament was against India. Different tournament and different venue but the same opponent and the same nemesis was to surface again for the Australians. It was the quarter-final match of the tournament and in a knock-out format, any team which lost would be packing its bags.

India batted first but found themselves in a corner when it lost its first two wickets for eight runs, including the one of Mohammad Azharuddin who didn't do justice to his 300th one-day international with a duck against his name. Tendulkar, in a nightmarish repeat for the Aussies, again assumed command and if anything, played better than he had all summer.

Bare statistics show that he had a 140-run third wicket stand with Rahul Dravid (48) and then a 132-run stand with vice-captain Ajay Jadeja (71) to put India past the 300-run mark. In reality, those who watched it were inclined to mark it down as the best ever effort yet by the master batsman. Unlike on previous occasions where he used to go hammer and tong at the bowlers, his response to the situation was more measured and assured. There was an inevitability about the way he went about his task: dominant yet serene and imperiously in control all through.

The first bout of aggression was witnessed in the 25th over by Brad Young, a young Australian medium-pacer. Tendulkar struck the first delivery over extra cover for six and then followed it up with another huge one over long off. The third was smashed past the infield for four and in all 19 runs came off the over. He then turned his attention to Kasprowicz, whose ability to reverse swing was considered a potent weapon on these pitches. The heavy-built Australian was milked for 71 runs in his 10 overs.

Tendulkar's century arrived in only 95 balls and after two in Sharjah, it was his third successive hundred against the

Australians. He didn't leave it at that and dazzled further before his innings was terminated at 141 by way of a run-out. It had taken him only 127 balls and contained 13 sweetly timed fours and three sixes.

The Australians were determined that they would not be beaten by one single man for the third time in a row. They were in no mood to pack up on their very first day of the tournament. Mark Waugh (74) was in one of his devastating moods and in company with Adam Gilchrist (26) and Ricky Ponting (41) provided the launch pad of 145 runs inside the first 25 overs.

Mohammad Azharuddin now turned to his golden boy to conjure up something out of the ordinary. Tendulkar's first over caused the spectators to sit up and take notice. His first couple of deliveries turned sharply enough to beat the bat and one wide apart, he conceded just four runs from it. It perked up the left-arm spinner Sunil Joshi at the other end who had Ponting out bowled. Brendon Julian was promoted up the order but the pinch-hitter was absolutely bewildered by Tendulkar's prodigious spin. He tried to take his chances against Joshi at the other end, belting him for a six and four, Mark Waugh fell to him, swinging across a straightish ball and an inside edge was accepted by the keeper.

Azhar dispensed with Tendulkar for a while but the opportunity was seized by Darren Lehmann to rehabilitate the Australian innings. Tendulkar was now brought in to replace Anil Kumble and it turned out to be a stroke of tactical genius. Steve Waugh holed out a return catch to Tendulkar and next at the crease was Michael Bevan. The presence of two left-handers at the crease didn't put off Tendulkar even though the pair was full of running, picking ones and twos. Tendulkar was now spinning it big and clean bowled Bevan in the 39th over.

Australia slipped further in the abyss when Lehmann was ruled out leg before to Ajit Agarkar by West Indian umpire Steve Bucknor, a marginal decision at best. Tendulkar, on a day when he could do nothing wrong, was mixing up his off and leg spinners with seamers slipped in between. He then cleaned up Damien Martyn and Brad Young to finish with figures of 4 for 38 in little more than nine overs. If his batting was not enough, it was Tendulkar the bowler who now caused Australia to come second best, losing the match by 44 runs. Tendulkar was to say later it was the best innings he had played in one-day cricket ever. "Everything I tried came off," he remembered "I had the complete measure of my strokeplay."

Despite Tendulkar's growing stature, the little master was still to strike an innings of mammoth proportion in one-day cricket. It was to arrive against New Zealand at home in Hyderabad in 1999, a few months after the fiasco of the World Cup in England where India just about managed to qualify for the Super Six stage and hardly looked a team worthy of being winners.

Indian cricket had undergone an upheaval of sorts after the World Cup. Mohammad Azharuddin was again the captain unwanted. There is something about England as far as Azhar's captaincy went. He lost it after the Indian tour to England in 1996 and now again he faced being sacked. The speculation grew that Tendulkar would once again captain his country. But the selectors were aware Tendulkar's first stint as captain had ended in disaster and the final few months of the reign were very bitter for him. He was never given his choices as captain and generally felt he was being tossed around. He didn't like the situation and with injuries to Javagal Srinath and Anil Kumble crippling his best chances in the West Indies and Sri Lanka in 1997, he had had enough of captaincy. Or so it seemed.

But now, after the 1999 World Cup, selectors were again looking up to Tendulkar to bail them out on the captaincy dilemma. It wasn't going to be easy and when Ajit Wadekar, chairman of the selection committee, sought him out for his views, Tendulkar categorically told him not to consider him for captaincy and let the other selectors know the same. Strangely, Wadekar never told his fellow selectors about Tendulkar's resolution and the others duly went ahead and announced Tendulkar as captain for the forthcoming home series against New Zealand.

Tendulkar, we are given to understand, was not the least amused by the development. He went into hiding and for a good couple of days, no-one had a clue of his whereabouts. The media were unable to get a statement from him and the suspense grew thicker because hints were dropped by those close to him that he would refuse the honour of leading the national side.

Indeed, to refuse or not to refuse was Tendulkar's dilemma. He must have had reason to feel done in by selectors, especially since he, on his part, had done enough to foretell them not to consider him. But now that they had gone ahead and named him as captain, refusing it would be tantamount to desertion of his duty in the eyes of millions and millions of Indian cricket fans. Many would dub him a traitor, a cricketer who doesn't have the larger interest of Indian cricket in mind and so on and so forth and Tendulkar was not prepared for such common perception. He has carefully sculpted his career as a smooth, line-free structure where controversy has no place to rest or be seen. He wasn't going to tar it now. But then he wasn't happy with the attitude of a few senior players in the side and didn't want to repeat the fiasco of 1997.

After due deliberations, Tendulkar emerged again in front of an adoring nation after spending a couple of days in a farmhouse. He apparently decided to accept the captaincy only after, one is given to understand, he had set out his conditions for it in front of the selectors and they decided to agree by it.

What were the conditions? There has never been an official statement from either the selectors or Tendulkar on the subject but the way his second tenure as captain went, apparently Mohammad Azharuddin and Nayan Mongia were not welcome in this team. Azharuddin, like all those cricketers who have been in control for a long period and then asked to play second fiddle to someone junior, largely sulked in 1997 and perhaps didn't give his full support to Tendulkar. Mongia was not forgiven, again one must believe, because many players in the team doubted his commitment. There is a famous story of how during their stand against Pakistan in the 1999 Chennai Test, Tendulkar would repeatedly ask Mongia to avoid playing lofted shots, or shots of danger, and yet when in sight of victory, the wicketkeeper batsman did exactly the same and was one of the reasons for India losing such a close game. It appears Tendulkar found it very difficult to forgive him.

Having secured Tendulkar's nod for captaincy, the selectors now went ahead and dropped Azhar and Mongia from the team. They also recalled India's cricketing legend Kapil Dev to be the coach of the team. Dev, who had largely looked after his business and spent his free time at the golf course, having had little to do since retiring in 1994, enjoyed nationwide popularity and in many ways had a bigger persona about him than even Tendulkar.

By the way Tendulkar began his second reign, it appeared he was keen to make amends for his failure during the first term. The first day in the office wasn't quite the way he wanted as India was shot out for 83 on a green top by New Zealand on the first day of the Mohali Test. Subsequently, India recovered to draw the Test, thanks to a hundred by Tendulkar, and then went on to win the series. Tendulkar carried his sublime form when the one-day series began and now crafted an innings of immense proportions.

It came during the second one-day international between the two teams in Hyderabad. India had lost the first game of the five-match series and another loss here would have set them back a long way. It was a good toss to win but the Indians lost Sourav Ganguly rather unfortunately when Tendulkar straight drove Shayne O' Connor who deflected it on to the non-striker's end to catch the former out of his ground.

From then on, it was batting mayhem at the Lal Bahadur Shastri Stadium in Hyderabad. Tendulkar and Rahul Dravid added 331 runs for the second wicket to push India to 376 for two in the 50 overs. Both recorded their highest ever one-day scores but Tendulkar came very close to overtaking all existing one-day individual batting marks. His unbeaten 186 was the fourth highest, after Pakistan's Saeed Anwar's 194, Viv Richards and Gary Kirsten's 188. Tendulkar's best till then was 143. Dravid helped himself to a total of 153 at a run-a-ball to improve upon his 145, scored during that record 318-run stand with Ganguly against Sri Lanka at Taunton during the 1999 World Cup.

It was a record which was put in shade by Tendulkar and Dravid at Hyderabad that day.

Tendulkar, as his score would convey, was unstoppable. There were orthodox drives and pulls interspersed with clever and hard running between the wickets. It drove the Kiwis to deep frustration as they could neither fall back completely in defence nor attack these two marauding batsmen enough. Tendulkar's knock from 151 balls contained 19 fours and four sixes while Dravid hammered 15 boundaries and two sixes during his innings. Their stand took 46.1 overs in the making. The last 10 overs yielded 133 runs, 28 of them in Chris Drum's last over, the innings 49th.

Tendulkar was within 12 runs of Anwar's 194 but the experienced Chris Cairns, bowling the final over, denied him the record. But it did enough to carry India to a total that was second only to Sri Lanka's 398 for five against Kenya in a 1996 World Cup match in Kandy.

The Kiwis, exasperated by the chase call, folded for 202 in the 34th over. Strangely, their run-rate was higher than India's through the length of their innings - only they kept losing wickets regularly.

For those interested in finding out how Tendulkar's second experiment with captaincy went, well, it wasn't much different than the disaster of the initial experience. India had a terrible time in Australia, losing the series 3-0 and the rival forces within the Board now created a situation which left Tendulkar with no option but to resign. They brought back Azhar and Mongia in the side.

That home series against South Africa would prove to be a cataclysmic one for world cricket. On a lower scale, India lost a home series for the first time in 14 years. On a much bigger scale, the Indian police would stumble on to a piece of evidence which would rip apart the mask of respectability from the game. The cricket world was rudely jolted to the reality of rampant match-fixing. Like 11/9 of recent times has redefined the political and social world order completely, this one would redraw the cricket boundaries forever.

THE RICHEST CRICKETER IN THE WORLD

Chances are, if you are at home or driving on the road in India, the smiling face of Tendulkar would accost you somehow. Better still, you happen to be pedalling away at a home-made bicycle in one of the dusty bylanes with open sewers overflowing - Tendulkar would still be around you. At home, you turn on the television or in office if you are catching up on the scores on the internet, a Tendulkar site would blip up and down to wean away your attention. It's like one of the sleazy dotcoms on the net, you open one and it won't allow you to go away all that easily. You close one and another would pop up and so on and so forth before you are finally broken away from the spell.

An interesting sight greeted one at Centurion Park in November 2001 when India were engaged in a five-day "unofficial" Test against South Africa. What could have been a match of immense interest, with India trailing one-nil in the series after having gallantly drawn the second at Port Elizabeth, the Centurion game turned out to be a damp squip because of match referee Mike Denness' decision to hand out punishment to six Indian players, including Tendulkar, during the previous game. The row soon engulfed the Indian cricket board and pitted it against the International Cricket Council (ICC), or more specifically Indian cricket supremo Jagmohan Dalmiya against the ICC president Malcolm Gray, and virtually brought the game to a standstill. The standoff caused what could have been a thriller at Centurion Park to be officially declared an "unofficial" Test.

The sightscreen at the far end had a digital advertisement on the entire length and breadth of it. It featured Italian automaker Palio's new budgeted small car at the bottom of the hoarding, with more than two-third of it being adorned by Tendulkar's face, giving a restrained even dignified smile. At the end of every over, with the striking batsman's back at the ubiquitous sightscreen, the Palio advertisement like a venetian blind would slowly open in front of a few

thousand spectators at Centurion Park - and in front of millions of television viewers in India and across the world.

Palio is only one of the latest to ride on the Tendulkar bandwagon of good image and high profile. He is the best known face in India, better than some of the superstars of Bollywood, India's Mumbai based film industry which produces more movies than even Hollywood, and a recent market survey suggested he enjoys more popularity than even the Prime Minister of India. Everything seems to be going for him: immensely successful and yet so young; a career unblemished by not even a hint of scandal (at a time when the match-fixing scandal was at its height Tendulkar was one of the rare few to avoid the scrutiny); an extremely dependable family man and a celebrity who espouses moral values rather than be a walking billboard for vulgar money. Money is important to him but not to the extent he compromises on his image or his privacy. Still, he happens to be the richest cricketer in the world.

If Tendulkar is cricket's most marketable commodity, the late Mark Mascarenhas was the one who created that profile. Mascarenhas was a large man and it must be said if cricket has become such a big marketable force in India - and the world - the bullish entrepreneur took a a chunk of credit as large as his own frame for it. He was born in Bangalore before he migrated to the United States and learnt his early marketing and business methods working for CBS before opening his own television company - WorldTel. His entry into the Indian cricket market in the mid-90s was fortuitous. Dalmiya was looking to take on the all-pervading presence of Doordarshan, India's state-owned television network, and sell cricket to the highest bidder. Doordarshan was a stumbling block and assumed unhindered access to cricket matches and telecasts as its birthright. It was seriously hampering Dalmiya's ambition to let market waves rule the cricket world. He wanted an outsider, a bull-in-a-china-shop kind of entity who would

shake up the system. It is all part of India's cricket history as to how Dalmiya and company got rid of Doordarshan's interfering presence from the cricket field; sold the 1996 World Cup to Mascarenhas and his WorldTel at a mind-boggling price and the association gradually spread to other countries, notably in Sri Lanka, Bangladesh and Sharjah. The world class quality telecast of matches, the burgeoning graph of one-day matches which converted millions and millions of neutrals into die-hard cricket fans, brought focus - and in its wake, money - like never before.

Mascarenhas, who liked being in the company of cricketers, then played a gamble which created a bigger stir and had his profile zooming further up on the horizon. WorldTel signed on the little genius Tendulkar for one and half million dollars annually for five years making him the most expensive cricketer ever. "It was a big risk," said WorldTel chief Mark Mascarenhas. "Somebody told me that he was available and that he wanted someone to represent him. I consulted people like Ravi Shastri and decided on signing the genius."

Till then Tendulkar, even though a major star and a captain-incumbent in 1995, was not such a hot property in the stakes of the advertising industry. His contract with Action Shoes, was worth a mere Rs 2 lakhs apparently. Even though cricket was popular, its visual appeal was greatly impaired by the poor quality of telecast from Doordarshan, and sponsors were few and far between. What also helped in cricket's image transformation was the fact that India was undergoing a major change in its political climate and for the first time in its history, had gone for open markets. It allowed foreign television networks and multi-national companies to make a pitch in India and cricket was a natural extension for this local and foreign business opportunity. Mascarenhas thus hedged his bets on Tendulkar and he didn't have any regrets. He acquired the right to market Tendulkar in 1996 for the guaranteed payment of $7.5 million (Rs 31.5 crores) over five years. In just under three years, WorldTel had raised $10 million (Rs 42 crores) in Tendulkar's name. Mascarenhas had after all backed a real star.

Tendulkar's rise coincided with the subcontinent's emergence as the commercial hub of world cricket. In 1992, the India rights for the World Cup were bought for Rs 25 lakh; for the 1996 World Cup it cost Rs 42 crore. Cricket became the national opiate. It meant that if Adidas pays Leander Paes Rs 12 lakh plus hefty bonuses, for Tendulkar it does not baulk at a crore and more per year in a six-year deal worth a couple of million dollars. Says G. Kannan, general manager, marketing, "At first glance it is a huge figure. But on analysis, if you look at his value, it appears reasonable." This is not a man to waste time bargaining over. During the 1996 World Cup, MRF representatives walked into Mascarenhas' room and said they wanted the rights to Tendulkar's bat. A deal was done in seconds.

The Mascarenhas-Tendulkar partnership grew at a definite pace till the former was killed in a car accident in western India early in 2002. Tendulkar got his respect and money from Mascarenhas even though the latter was not liked by everyone because of his bullish, even boorish, behaviour at times. Mascarenhas in due course of time would also be investigated for his allegedly dubious role in television contracts which now of course has little meaning. Many associated with the game couldn't bring themselves to accept the alliance of somebody as clean as Tendulkar with somebody as uproarious as Mascarenhas.

So when the time for Tendulkar's renewal of contract came up in 2000, there were many who were willing to throw their hats in the ring and see if Tendulkar would catch the bait. They assumed Tendulkar would distance himself from Mascarenhas, as he had done to Ajay Jadeja, one of his real pals before the match-fixing disclosures dragged the latter in its pit. Tendulkar, against the sentiments of many, walked ahead and signed another deal with Mascarenhas.

The money promised by Mascarehas to Tendulkar was huge even outrageous. He assured Tendulkar of a sum of Rs 100 crores over the next five years, a figure which matched what the accounts of the Indian cricket board showed as profit for its massive operations. Mascarenhas badly needed a prop to help his sagging image in the changed scenario of a new century and his hold on the game had largely come unstuck. He was bailed out by Tendulkar who lent his own reputation to save the one of his long-time manager. It gave Mascarenhas a certain respectability, a kind of lifeline, and showed Tendulkar loyalty to his mates of standing. Under the new contract, Tendulkar would be paid Rs 20 crores per annum for the next five years from WorldTel - while his annual match fees would not exceed Rs 60 lakhs!

Tendulkar has already signed on with Britannia, HomeTrade, Boost, MRF, Adidas, Visa, Pepsi and more recently Fiat Palio. Each of these contracts is said to average about Rs 1.5 crore a year. Sources say that for HomeTrade, he was paid a whopping Rs 5 crore. A fast-food chain of stores across the world was also being planned by Mascarenhas to capitalise on Tendulkar's image before his death put the matter on hold.

Tendulkar brings his own clinical efficiency for his sponsors off the field. He is known to refuse a cola in public and insists on Pepsi which he endorses. This story would help drive the point home: Recently he was travelling on a private airline and was offered a cola by an airhostess. He politely turned it down and asked for Pepsi. A fellow passenger, impressed by the icon's brand loyalty, conveyed this to Vibha Paul Rishi, executive vice-president (marketing) of Pepsi, who interacts with Tendulkar on the company's behalf. Rishi dashed off a letter thanking Tendulkar. The little genius' response was typical: "You can always expect that from me." "That's typical Sachin," said Vibha "It's pretty hard initially to get him to sign up for you. But once he does, he is totally committed to the product."

In fact the four major sponsors of Sachin, MRF, Grindlays and adidas, apart from Pepsi, whom The Wee - a national magazine, spoke to were quick to commend his commitment. "We were to shoot a commercial with Sachin at the end of a very tiring day," reminisced G. Kannan, general manager (marketing), adidas. "His commitment while doing the shoot was incredible."

Alok Jetley, director (card sales and marketing), Grindlays Bank, had a similar experience. "Sachin had just returned from a long overseas trip when he arrived at our shoot," he recalled. "Yet he patiently worked with our team."

"He is accommodating and easy to communicate with," said Rodrigues, general manager (advertising), MRF. And it is not one or two stray incidents that prove his loyalty to the people who pay him. Deepak Jolly, vice-president (corporate communication) of Pepsi, related another incident. "Pepsi's association with Sachin started in 1993," he said. "He was definitely a good player then but not a superstar. In 1997 we did not extend the contract. In 1998 we again approached him and the fact that we had first signed him even when he was not a superstar was very much there in his mind. He agreed to sign up with us again. He is not a person to sell his loyalty."

But why did these companies opt for Sachin in the first place? The fact that he is the best cricketer in the world today is an obvious reason. But it is Sachin's off-the-field demeanour that makes him a complete role model.

"When we talk of Sachin as a role model we are not talking of his cricket," said Jolly "It is the way he has handled his success. It hasn't changed the way he lives. It is the strong principles and values he holds in spite of his amazing success that we are going to highlight in the future." In fact the Pepsi ad which shows Sachin playing cricket with the boys on the street was an attempt by the cola company to bring out his qualities as a person.

Alok had a number of reasons to explain why Grindlays signed Sachin. "He is hard-working, committed, a family person, intelligent, thoughtful, widely recognised yet approachable and friendly. This is what our target prospect aspires for and identifies with," he explained.

His views are echoed by Kannan. "He may not be the most flashy person around but he certainly represents the right values that we want to be associated with," he said. "He is just far ahead of the rest."

Tendulkar has personal sponsorship worth US$15.5 million over four years with companies such as Philips, MRF, Colgate, Adidas, Visa and Pepsi. Tendulkar is paid $15,000 for each Test match appearance and $6,000 for a limited overs international. Everytime he hits a century for India, Pepsi tops up his pocket money with another $15,000. His souvenir bat recently fetched $1500. Compared to Tendulkar, Viswanathan Anand, India's celebrated chess star, made just around Rs 5 crore through his endorsement of computer education company NIIT. According to industry sources, Anand's match fees are two to five times higher than what cricketers in India draw.

Anand's appearance fees range from $100,000 (Rs 47 lakh) to $250,000 (Rs 1.2 crore) per event. Anand earned $660,000 (Rs 3.1 crore) when he became world champion in December 2000.

A distant number three and four are Sourav Ganguly and Rahul Dravid. Industry estimates indicate that the Indian cricket captain has earned approximately Rs 4.5 crore from his international cricketing career while deputy Dravid would have made Rs 4.2 crore.

Endorsements of course are very much part of the game. Ganguly has been featuring in campaigns ranging from the soft drink Coke to the two-wheeler giant Hero Honda. Dravid endorses Pepsi and Kissan Jammy as well as Castrol. Tendulkar fills a vacuum in a nation bereft of role models, in and beyond sport. He has an appeal that is seductive to the entire Indian universe. "Audiences are fragmented, but he's one of the few big unifying symbols," says Rajan. It is an aura so compelling that one sponsor admits: "If you put him on one side and the team on the other, he is still the meatier proposition." A recent TNT/Cartoon Network poll among 600 children in the 7-18 age-group endorses that. When they were asked to name India's top sportsperson, Sachin received 51 per cent of the vote; Mohammed Azharuddin was a distant second at 10 per cent. Predictably, no Indian cricketer is paid close to Rs 1 crore a year; only Australia's Shane Warne, signed on by Nike and Channel Nine, is endorsed so heavily.

Tendulkar has cultivated his image sensibly. Unafraid of interviews, careful not to court controversy, he is, says sports entrepreneur Lokesh Sharma, "a winner with the boy-next-door face". He will never earn what basketball icon Michael Jordan does, yet he escapes the censure Jordan faces. As the American writer Frank Deford put it, "This Jordan is a conglomerate, they say, too greedy, lacking social responsibility."

Tendulkar is a mini-conglomerate. More comfortably, social consciousness is not a required part of his agenda. Quietly, one hears, he does his part, like assisting a programme that helps Mumbai slum children. But Indians, interested only in what he does at the wicket, do not quibble over how much he earns. Why should they? When last could one man alone lift a nation's mood?

THE ESSENTIAL TENDULKAR

To those who know Tendulkar, his greatest strength is his uncommon courtesy to all. It stands to reason he probably has no option but to do so lest he hurts the sentiments of millions of his adoring fans and to keep the prying media in humour. But when the same decency is extended to his colleagues and opponents on the field of play, it points to an amazingly civilized spirit of the man. This is not new for the man. Indeed, Tendulkar's public face has been the same since fame and popularity sought him out at the tender age of 16 years.

A careful scrutiny would reveal in all these years hardly anyone had anything bad to say about Tendulkar. A Sunil Gavaskar would raise the ire of a few with his sharp remarks and a certain moodiness; A Bishan Bedi wears his tongue on his sleeve; a Steve Waugh would rail you, at least in his formative years, with his antics and pungent remarks; a Viv Richards would cause arrogance to seep into his demeanour sometimes; Ian Botham and Shane Warne would have their indiscretions; a Wasim Akram and Waqar Younis or an Imran Khan and Sarfraz Nawaz would fight public battles; Martin Crowe and Glenn Turner would show more than a generation gap to the world; but with Tendulkar there is no spice accompanying the tale.

Two incidents though came very close to dragging Tendulkar's good name through the mud. One of course was the ball-tampering punishment which match referee Mike Denness handed out to him during the Port Elizabeth Test of India's South African tour in 2001-2. And the second concerned, again, the ball-tampering allegation which Abdur Razzaq, Pakistan's rising all-rounder, cast at him during a one-day game of the Carlton and United series in Australia during the 2000-2001 series.

Denness' action was open to question on many fronts. One, he should have informed the two umpires in the middle on his walkie-talkie to have a ball inspection done at a drinks interval which was only a few overs away; he should have also seen through the umpteen replays to realise Tendulkar didn't have nails at all when the camera caught him working on the ball. Denness didn't do his image much good when after all the storm had died down, he let the world know that even he didn't think the ball had been tampered with. It must be said though, as Sunny Gavaskar rightly pointed out, Tendulkar was technically at fault because the rule book clearly state only "working or cleaning" of the ball must be done in the presence of the umpires. Tendulkar didn't do so but to accuse a man of ball-tampering when he bowls five or six overs at the most and that too not at medium-pace was carrying justice too far.

Razzaq's incident was still more curious. India was already out of the triangular series for all intent and purposes yet the Pakistani cricketer chose to go hard at a few senior Indian cricketers, including Tendulkar. Apparently, he did so at the insistence of his manager. The manager did confide to yours truly after Razzaq had gone ahead and complained to the two umpires against Tendulkar. "He (Razzaq) did something stupid. Actually the boys had complained in previous games that the Indians were sledging a lot on the field. I just asked them to give it back. But for Razzaq to suggest something as outrageous as ball-tampering by Tendulkar was stupid. As a punishment, I would not field him in the next game." Sure enough, Razzaq didn't play the next game. Kapil Dev, the Indian team's manager was livid. "One can understand if he did something like this to others but to Tendulkar who has a spotless image in the game is incredulous".

Tendulkar's response to both these incidents was to keep his cool and not join the battle. So assured is the man of his innate dignity, he allowed a certain lapse of time to do justice to the issue. Sure enough, the charges didn't stick. Today, not many in the game think Tendulkar tampered with the ball. Tendulkar stood his ground, not by speaking but by keeping silent. Silence, if properly used, can be evocative as we all know.

Tendulkar must have upset a few cricketers during his long career. Two names which come readily to mind are those of Mohammad Azharuddin and Nayan Mongia. Azhar lost his captaincy to Tendulkar and showed his bitterness by being unco-operative in team affairs. Tendulkar's response in a similar situation was to produce his best year ever in 1998 and win trophies galore for the team and the nation. Mongia, common perception has it, didn't enjoy the confidence of Tendulkar. Both of these cricketers were not picked in the squad when Tendulkar lead a team to Australia for a series in 2000-2001. Yet, after they lost their berths and then found themselves neck deep in the match-fixing storm thereafter, both Azhar and Mongia carried little ammunition in their barrel to fire at Tendulkar.

In India's recent series against England at home, the media reported the verbal exchanges between Tendulkar and Nasser Hussain. It was believed since left-arm spinner Ashley Giles was pitching it way beyond the leg-stump to stop run-scoring by Tendulkar, having the batsman frustrated, it spilled over into an exchange between the two cricketers. Tendulkar's explanation to this is interesting. Apparently, Giles' method wasn't the issue. Hussain was being plainly rude to Shiv Sunder Das, the non-striker, as his position at the other end wasn't quite suiting Giles' approach to his bowling crease. Apparently Hussain used language which wasn't acceptable. Tendulkar intervened and got abused in return. At the end of the day though Tendulkar still had only good things to say about Hussain. "He is a very fine captain, I think," was all one could get Tendulkar to say on Hussain.

Tendulkar has often said the ideal balance for a batsman to achieve would be to have the unwavering concentration of a Sunil Gavaskar to go with the attacking instincts of a Viv Richards. Despite belonging to Mumbai where very few batsmen have escaped not being influenced by Gavaskar, it must be said the essential Tendulkar is vastly different from the legendary opener. Tendulkar forces bowlers to err, while Gavaskar used to wait for them to tire. Then again, they batted at different positions and need not be compared carefully.

Though Sir Donald Bradman always likened Tendulkar's batting to his own when alive, it must be said the latter looked up to Richards when young. Tendulkar was thrilled when he met Viv in person at the Commonwealth Games in

Kuala Lumpur Malaysia in 1998. He was also mightily impressed with Sri Lanka's Sanath Jayasuriya who plundered runs by the hundreds against India in 1997. I haven't seen Sir Don, but I have seen Jayasuriya," was how Tendulkar described the mercurial left-hander.

Still, it isn't if Tendulkar would not try to disturb a batsman's rhythm at the crease. If a few chosen words would do the trick, he is game. But he isn't an outrageous sledger as many others are in international cricket. There is this famous story of how Tendulkar was badly sledged by the Waugh brothers in Sydney 1992. Ravi Shastri was Tendulkar's senior partner and remembers how the latter would vow between overs to teach his opponents a lesson after he had carried India to safety. Tendulkar only toughens up when cornered and international teams prefer not to sledge him at the crease these days.

Tendulkar is not a mediaperson's delight for sure. Unless you are a statistician that is, counting up all his hundreds and thousands of runs and all those fours and sixes. Tendulkar would hardly give you good copy and unfailingly supported his men when he was captain. The only instance one remembers when he lost his cool was in Pakistan after a one-day game in 1997. A scribe was to ask how Kumble, who was in the middle of a terrible bowling slump, could be persisted with in the team when he hardly spun the ball. Tendulkar, with an edge in his voice, shot back. "Do you know how many wickets Kumble has taken? Do you have any idea?" One hasn't seen Tendulkar lose his shirt in public but the master batsman says when he loses his temper, people prefer to stay away. "But I don't think anyone has seen me get angry," remarks Tendulkar.

His critics say he tends to hang around with his Mumbai mates only. That's true only if it concerns leaving for a party or for food when on a tour. But otherwise it is unlikely a young Indian cricketer would have a complaint of inattention against Tendulkar. He went out of his way to promote talents from other states in India when he was in charge of the team. Punjab's Vikram Rathore was backed even when the bearded batsman was suffering failures in the mid 90s. He was fully behind Harbhajan Singh when the off-spinner was traumatised with the chucking issue. Indeed team coach John Wright usually leaves it for Tendulkar to devote his attention to the younger men, giving them catching practice and ironing out flaws, if any, in their batting.

Critics point out that despite his brilliance, Tendulkar hasn't won many Tests for India. India continues to struggle to win Tests abroad - indeed the country has only five overseas wins to show in nearly 80 years of Test history. There have been innings, like the 155 against Australia at Chennai in 1998, which were match-defining yet somehow Tendulkar hasn't played an innings which Brian Lara and Steve Waugh have occasionally produced in their careers. He is conscious of it and says it is something he would like to improve upon in coming days. It probably has led to a revision of his batting methods. He no longer is inclined to hit in the air a great deal. Instead, he tries to use the gaps and place the ball in the field to keep his score mounting.

Too often Tendulkar in the past has caused his downfall by reaching out for wide deliveries and hitting over the top. Now there is a re-evaluation of his methods. He knows despite a few brilliant batters in the eleven, the team depends on him to play a guiding role. He probably has also heard someone like Wasim Akram who criticises the over-dependence of the Indian team on Tendulkar.

"We always got the impression that Tendulkar's success and failure translated into his team's fortunes. If you could get Tendulkar out cheaply, the rest looked demoralised and ready to be rolled over. We used this tactic successfully during the 1998-1999 tour to India. It must be causing enormous pressure on Tendulkar," said Wasim.

Tendulkar feels that he enjoys such pressure as it brings the best out of him. He still doesn't sleep on the eve of a Test. He has been around for over a dozen years yet he tosses around in his bed before a Test gets going. "I am tense before an innings but as soon as I step out and take guard in the middle, I am relaxed," he said recently. Bowlers in recent years have tried to pitch it way beyond the leg-stump curling it enough to hit his pads. England, in a recent series, were on a Tendulkar mission. Medium-pacers would hurl the ball full but too wide outside the off-stump while left-arm spinners would pitch it way beyond the leg-stump, curling it enough not to be called a wide. Tendulkar finds his own way to deal with such tactics. When he found Sanath Jayasuriya doing so in Sri Lanka in 1997, he started that paddle sweep of his where the ball doesn't get an angle from the bat but generally is helped along the same route behind the keeper to fine leg. Now with a fielder being stationed there, that opportunity is being restricted.

Tendulkar's response to similar tactics by Zimbabwe's Raymond Price in a recent home series was to even reverse sweep the left-arm spinner for four. Sourav Ganguly was amazed by the shot. "It wasn't a reverse sweep as such but a full and proper stroke in which he changed the position of his hands on the handle." Could one see Tendulkar playing more of these strokes in future? "Not in Tests," confides Tendulkar "It is too risky a stroke to be played in a Test match."

Tendulkar says all these years of travelling and playing matches hasn't diluted his intensity. Indeed, he is more than ever determined to complete a few unfinished jobs. One suspects it includes winning matches for India, playing less in the air and staying longer at the wicket. In the recent series against England and Zimbabwe, he was more than willing to stick around and generally looked to bat for over six-hour stints in the middle. All this can only mean further bad news for the bowlers.

" T H I S   M A N   I S   A   L E G E N D "

His shot selection is superb, he just lines you up and can make you look very silly. Everything is right in his technique and judgement. There isn't a fault there. He is also a lovely guy, and over the years I've enjoyed some interesting chats with him...Sachin is in a different class to Lara as a professional cricketer. He is a model cricketer, and despite the intolerable pressures he faces back home, he remains a really nice guy... Sachin is also the best batsman in the world, pulling away from Brian Lara every year...We'd heard all about him modelling himself on Sunil Gavaskar, and he had the same neatness, the same time to spare, the same calmness - and a very heavy bat. **Allan Donald**

Tendulkar is the best in the world at the moment. Why I've always liked him is that batsmen tend to be negative at times and I think batting is not about not getting out - it is to play positively. I think you got to take it to the bowlers and Sachin is one such player. When you do so, you change the game, you change bowlers because they suddenly start bowling badly because they are under pressure. **Graeme Pollock**

You take Don Bradman away and he is next up, I reckon.
Steve Waugh

The thing I like the most about Sachin is his intensity. After being in the game for so long, he still has the same desire to do well for India in any international match. I tell you what, this man is a legend. **Sourav Ganguly**

Eleven years ago when he first played against us in Pakistan, I remember (Imran) telling us this youngster (Tendulkar) is destined for big things. Imran took an immense liking to the determined youngster and I think he (Tendulkar) has not really disappointed in fulfiling his potential. I would have loved to bowl to him in my prime say six years ago. I could not do that because of the tense cricket relations between Pakistan and India. It is one of the biggest regrets of my cricket career. But the last time I bowled to him in a Test was in 1999 in India and he clearly showed his class on a few occasions. To me he is the complete batsman. What has

impressed me most about him is his focus and determination to do well. I think the youngsters can learn a lot from just watching him play and emulating his determination. Despite being so immensely gifted, he is still so determined to excel every time he goes out to bat for his country, it is something I have always respected.
Wasim Akram

They (Bradman and Tendulkar) looked pretty much identical. You could not avoid the feeling that part of Bradman was there in Tendulkar. **Rodney Marsh**

I think there are some in this world who would find fault even with the best. This guy has scored over 10,000 runs or thereabouts in both forms of cricket but he is still criticised. It just amazes me. **Kapil Dev**

He is like a god in India
Matthew Hayden

The thing I admire most about this man is his poise. The way he moves, elegantly without ever looking out of place in any condition or company, suggests his pedigree. I remember he had once come to New Delhi in the 1990s to collect his Arjuna Award (India's highest award to its top sportspersons) and he asked me if I would attend the function. He is a very sensitive human being... Sometimes you feel he really hasn't felt the kind of competition in the world his talent deserves. I would have loved to see him perform against top quality cricketers of the previous generation. It would really have brought out the best in him.
Bishan Singh Bedi

In the early years, especially around the mid 90s, I had this feeling you could play around on his ego and get him out. He believed he could attack bowlers at any time and anyone who could bowl maidens to him stood a good chance. Things are of course different now. **Erapalli Prasanna**

Tendulkar is the best batsman of the world - on par with Steve Waugh. **Glenn McGrath**

The more I see him, the more I want to see him
Mohammad Azharuddin

...On the eve of his departure to England in 1990, I had been invited by the other residents of the co-operative society where he lived (then) to be the Chief Guest at the good luck farewell function they were having for him. I remember saying then, that his voice (it still does) sounded like Sir Don Bradman's and I hoped that he would be able to do a bit like Sir Don did on his first tour of England. At that time Sachin did not even have a Test century to his name and there were some, who thought I was getting a bit carried away. India's fortune will depend on how many runs the little champion scores. There is no doubt Tendulkar is the real thing. **Sunil Gavaskar**

I'd like to see him go out one day and bat with a stump. I tell you he'd do OK...I just get the feeling because of his mental strength that Sachin will be definitely the best player of his era and probably the best 2-3 of all time. **Greg Chappell**

Much has been made of my personal contest with Tendulkar. Some people have said that my duel with Tendulkar in India in 1997-98 was the most compelling Test cricket they have ever seen, but there is no doubt he enjoyed the better of the exchanges... He has played me better than anybody. Most Indian batsmen pick the length very quickly, even when it is flighted above the eyeline, but Tendulkar moved into position even earlier than the likes of Mohammad Azharuddin and Rahul Dravid... His footwork is immaculate. He would either go right forward or all the way back and he has the confidence to go for his strokes... Although my statistics in that series don't make happy reading, I am still prepared to say it was a pleasure to bowl to him...Obviously I never bowled to the Don, but if he was consistently superior to Tendulkar then I am glad he was an Australian.
Shane Warne

We always knew that Sachin Tendulkar was a great cricketer, but after the Coca-Cola Cup (Sharjah, 1998), we have seen the birth of a legend. I can't think of anybody who has batted more authoritatively in one day cricket for India, or even in the world except for Viv Richards...He is someone sent from up there to play cricket and go back. **Ravi Shastri**

I can't dream of an innings like that. He exists where we can't.
Ajay Jadeja, Sharjah in 1998

Playing in the same team as Sachin is a huge honour. His balance of mind, shrewd judgement, modesty and, above all, his technical brilliance make him my all-time hero... You can't get a more complete cricketer than Sachin. He has everything that a cricketer needs to have. As a batsman, he has the technique, the hunger and the desire for runs. He always contributes with the bat as well as on the field. He also is a good fielder and bowls when needed. You really can't ask for a better cricketer than Sachin...He is a terrific person and has handled pressure brilliantly. He has handled his success very well and doesn't have any airs about him. He is a great guy and very good team man. In his heart of hearts, he is a very simple and down to earth person.
Rahul Dravid

His mind is like a computer. He stores data on bowlers and knows where they are going to pitch the ball.
Navjot Singh Sidhu

A complete batsman - he's the best in the business.
Mohinder Amarnath

I think he's marvellous. I think he will fit in whatever category of cricket that's been played or will be played, from the first ball that's ever been bowled to the last ball that's going to be. He can play in any era and at any level... What he looks to do first is to attack. If it's not there in the groove he waits for the line and defends. Most of the time batsmen, just because it could be a fearsome fast bowler they are facing, tend to defend. But Sachin's

always ready. He's always in a position to take advantage of loose balls...He has something special. He's blessed...I would say he's 99.5 per cent perfect...Even if he retires tomorrow and doesn't achieve anything more he is right there...I have never seen Bradman but heard people talk about him. But I tell you what, if Bradman could bat like this man does then he was dynamite. Players like Sachin deserve to be preserved in cotton wool.
Viv Richards

You might pitch a ball on the off stump and think you have bowled a good ball and he walks across and hits it for two behind midwicket. His bat looks so heavy but he just waves it around like it's a toothpick. **Brett Lee**

First and foremost, Tendulkar is an entertainer and that for me is as important factor as any fact or figure. Too often boring players have been pushed forward as great by figures alone. For sheer entertainment, he will keep cricket alive.
Barry Richards

Neil Harvey, Sunny, all had the footwork and the judgement. With Sachin his stroke off the backfoot, particularly off the pace bowler, is extraordinary - the next thing you know is that someone is picking the ball up from the gutter.
Richie Benaud

He is a genius. He has a shot for every ball. The only way to stop him is to keep him off strike. **Wes Hall**

Everytime I see him he gets better, his concentration reminds me of Sunny. **Ian Botham**

For Sachin the balance is there. He is quick to complete his shot. He covers the crease much better than mere mortals.
David Gower

Whenever I see Sachin play I am reminded of the Graeme Pollock quote of Cricket being a 'see the ball, hit the ball game.' He hits the ball if the it's there to be hit.
Ian Chappell

What we should do is enjoy Sachin's batting while we can. His wicket will be the biggest prize sought after by every bowler around the world. That has always been the case for batsmen who hold the mantle of 'best in the world'
Geoff Boycott

Sachin is a genius. I'm a mere mortal.
Brian Lara

I reckon he'll play another eight to 10 years and I would be surprised if he doesn't get more than 40 centuries.. During the 90s, Brian Lara, Inzamam-ul-Haq and yours truly have often been spoken of as the best in the batting business along with Tendulkar... However, I would rate Tendulkar higher than the rest. Lara comes close because he's a proven match-winner, but he does give the opposition chances... Tendulkar is technically superior, has every stroke in the book and some of his own, and above all is remarkably consistent...I'm not in the same class as him...The pressure on me is nothing compared to Sachin Tendulkar. He, like God, must never fail. The crowd always expects him to succeed and it is too much pressure on him.
Mark Waugh

He has never been in a hurry. His basics are strong and he thrives on that. He is always calm and cool , but at the same time does not allow the bowlers to prevail over him. He is very gutsy... I have known him since he was 10 years old and also would like to tell you that I know him better than anybody else. He is a gem of a person. He is always helpful and co-operative. He is responsible and always finds time to spend with the family. I don't see any change in his behaviour. He is the same Sachin whom I met years ago. Success has not gone into his head. He is down to earth.
Vinod Kambli

I am very privileged to have played with him and seen most of the runs that he has scored. I am also extremely happy to have shared the same dressing room... He is a very reserved person and generally keeps to himself. He is very determined, committed and doesn't show too many emotions. He just goes about doing his job. **Anil Kumble**

Sachin is a gem of a person. He has a very positive attitude. Everybody in the team wants to win, but I guess Sachin wants to win more than anybody else. **Robin Singh**

He is stupendous. I don't want to run out of adjectives describing him. **Anshuman Gaekwad**

I saw him playing on television and was struck by his technique, so I asked my wife to come look at him. Now I never saw myself play, but I feel that this player is playing much the same as I used to play, and she looked at him on television and said yes, there is a similarity between the two..his compactness, technique, stroke production..it all seemed to gel! **Sir Don Bradman**

Technically he stands out as the best because of his ability to increase the pace at will. **David Boon**

Sachin is an attacker. He has much more power than Sunny. He wants to be the one to set the pace. He has to be on top. That's the buzz about him. **Jeff Thomson**

If I'm to bowl to Sachin, I'll bowl with my helmet on. He hits the ball so hard. **Dennis Lillee**

I'll be going to bed having nightmares of Sachin just running down the wicket and belting me back over the head for six...I don't think anyone, apart from Don Bradman, is in the same class as Sachin Tendulkar. He is just an amazing player. **Shane Warne**

It was one of the greatest innings I have ever seen. There is no shame being beaten by such a great player, Sachin is perhaps only next to the Don.
Steve Waugh, Sharjah in 1998

Hell if he stayed, even at 11 an over he would have got it...It's scary. Where the hell do we bowl to him...Imagine what he'll be like when he is 28.
Allan Border, Sharjah (final) in 1998

He's a phenomenon We have tried to be switched on when he plays, allow him no boundaries, for then he doesn't stop.
Mark Taylor

Tendulkar is the most complete batsman I have stood behind. I saw the hundred in Perth on a bouncy pitch with Hughes, McDermott and Whitney gunning for him - he only had 60-odd when the No. 11 came in. **Ian Healy**

Sachin's undoubtedly no. 1 today but I wouldn't start comparing him with Viv Richards till he scores hundreds against quality fast bowlers on fast pitches. **Michael Holding**

He is a tremendous cricketer. He is young and has got a lot of ability. He's got his own style. He has got the temperament for big cricket and I hope that he goes from strength to strength.
Clive Lloyd

In an over I can bowl six different balls. But then Sachin looks at me with a sort of gentle arrogance down the pitch as if to say 'Can you bowl me another one?'
Adam Hollioake

He has given a new dimension to batting. Such dominance can break the heart of the best of bowlers. I was never tired of watching this wonderful batsman
Asif Iqbal

Test cricket Record

To April 1st 2002

Batting

Versus	M	Inns	NO	50s	100s	HS	Runs	Avg	Sa	St
Australia	15	28	2	5	6	177	1406	54.08	8	0
Bangladesh	1	1	0	0	0	18	18	18.00	0	0
England	12	18	2	6	5	177	1282	80.13	13	0
New Zealand	12	19	5	3	3	217	891	63.64	7	0
Pakistan	7	12	0	2	1	136	395	32.92	1	0
South Africa	14	26	1	3	3	169	948	37.92	10	0
Sri Lanka	13	16	2	3	6	148	1124	80.29	8	0
West Indies	8	12	1	5	1	179	691	62.82	10	0
Zimbabwe	9	14	2	3	3	201★	918	76.50	5	0
Overall	**91**	**146**	**15**	**30**	**28**	**217**	**7673**	**58.57**	**62**	**0**

Test cricket Record

To April 1st 2002

Bowling

Versus	O	M	R	W	Best	Avg	S/R	E/R
Australia	106.2	16	339	8	3/31	42.38	79.75	3.19
Bangladesh	10	2	34	1	1/34	34.00	60.00	3.40
England	30	6	88	1	2/27	88.00	180.00	2.93
New Zealand	30	6	98	4	2/7	24.50	45.00	3.27
Pakistan	20	2	88	4	2/35	22.00	30.00	4.40
South Africa	42.4	7	138	5	3/10	27.60	51.20	3.25
Sri Lanka	16	4	29	0				1.81
West Indies	6	0	28	0				4.67
Zimbabwe	62	15	172	2	1/19	86.00	186.00	2.77
Overall	**323.0**	**58**	**1014**	**25**	**3/10**	**40.56**	**77.52**	**3.14**

One Day International Record

To April 1st 2002

Batting

Versus	M	Inns	NO	50s	100s	HS	Runs	Avg	Sa	St
Australia	33	33	0	7	6	143	1626	49.27	17	0
Bangladesh	6	5	0	1	0	54	199	39.80	2	0
England	20	20	2	4	0	91	650	36.11	9	0
Kenya	8	7	3	0	4	146	559	139.75	1	0
New Zealand	31	30	1	7	3	186*	1279	44.10	5	0
Pakistan	43	41	4	9	2	118	1335	36.08	25	0
South Africa	40	40	0	5	3	122	1310	32.75	7	0
Sri Lanka	45	43	5	9	6	137	1760	46.32	15	0
United Arab Em	1	1	0	1	0	63	63	63.00	1	0
West Indies	29	29	6	8	2	122*	1046	45.48	6	0
Zimbabwe	30	29	6	4	5	146	1242	54.00	5	0
Overall	**286**	**278**	**27**	**55**	**31**	**186***	**11069**	**44.10**	**93**	**0**

One Day International Record

To April 1st 2002

Bowling

Versus	O	M	R	W	Best	Avg	S/R	E/R
Australia	135.1	1	645	18	5/32	35.83	45.06	4.77
Bangladesh	16.3	0	78	5	2/8	15.60	19.80	4.79
England	59.5	0	326	2	1/30	163.00	179.50	5.48
Kenya	18	0	112	0				6.22
New Zealand	108.3	3	540	13	3/34	41.54	50.08	4.99
Pakistan	140.4	1	725	13	3/45	55.77	64.92	5.16
South Africa	171	4	843	13	4/56	64.85	78.92	4.93
Sri Lanka	134.5	4	615	15	3/43	41.00	53.93	4.57
United Arab Em	5	0	22	0				4.40
West Indies	118	6	514	16	4/34	32.13	44.25	4.36
Zimbabwe	92.2	0	530	10	1/6	53.00	55.40	5.75
Overall	**999.5**	**19**	**4950**	**105**	**5/32**	**47.14**	**57.13**	**4.95**